Years of Challenge and Change: An Autobiography

God Answers Prayer while Time Changes Things

Answorth Hervan Moitt

Copyright © 2019 by Answorth Hervan Moitt.

Cover: concept and design by A.H.M. Moitt

ISBN   Softcover   978-1-950580-24-8

All rights reserved. No part of this book may be reproduced or transmitted in any form or by any means, electronic or mechanical, including photocopying, recording, or by any information storage and retrieval system without express written permission from the author, except in the case of brief quotations embodied in critical reviews and certain other non-commercial uses permitted by copyright law.

Scripture and Versions used by permission

Scriptures taken from the Holy Bible New International Version® Copy Wright1984 by Biblica Inc. Used by permission of Zondervan. All rights reserved worldwide.

Scriptural quotations are from Common Bible New Revised Standard Version® of the Bible. Copyright 1973 National Council of Churches of Christ in United States of America. Used by permission. All rights reserved.

Scriptures taken from old and new King James Version ® 1924, 1984 respectively. By Thomas Nelson Used by permission. All rights reserved.

Printed in the United States of America.

To order additional copies of this book, contact:
Bookwhip
1-855-339-3589
https://www.bookwhip.com

Table of Contents

About The Author v

About the Book vii

Book Reviewed ix

Dedications xi

Introduction xiii

Chapter One
I Prayed for Healing and He Gave me Time 1

Chapter Two
Prayed for Healing and He Gave me an Education 14

Chapter Three
I Prayed for Healing and He Gave me a Wife 29

Chapter Four
I Prayed for Healing and He Gave me a College Degree 45

Chapter Five
I Prayed for Healing and He Gave me a Grand Opportunity 79

Chapter Six
I Prayed for Healing and God gave me a New Fellowship . . .122

Chapter Seven
I Prayed for Healing and He Gave me an Open Future 150

Storyline through Photos 157

About The Author

Answorth Hervan Mackenzie Moitt's character is strong in determination; thinks strategically; is self-motivated, with superb integrity. He was birthed on January 18th 1952, on the small but exquisitely beautiful island of Antigua in the West Indies. He is the seventh of ten children born to his mother and the eleventh of his father's sixteen. Both worked to support growing families. He has had an international education: earned a diploma in Theology at West Indies Theological College, Port-of-Spain, Trinidad; earned a Master of Divinity at School of Theology, Anderson University, Anderson, Indiana; Associate of Arts in Education at Miami-Dade College, Miami, Florida; Bachelor of Science in Elementary Education and Master of Science in Reading Education respectively from Barry University, Miami Shores, Florida.

Answorth was ordained in 1990 and served as pastor of Zion Church of God, Antigua, from 1987-1990.

He and his family answered the call to serve the Tottenham Community Church of God in London, England, 1995-2001. On completion of ministry there, the family returned to Miami, Florida, 2002, where he planted and pastored the now closed Homestead Community Church of God from 2005-2016.

Answorth is a lover of good humor and comedy. In music, he cherishes classical oratorios such as the Handel Messiah, Elijah and Joseph; old and new gospel songs, as well as the West Indian expressions of the steel band, Reggae and Calypso. For Reggae and Calypso songs, his preferences are those with lyrics of social commentary that helps to awaken and strengthen consciousness of equity and justice within the community. One might even go to the length of saying that the singers of such lyrics are our modern-day prophets. In film, he likes epics/historical drama, action, adventure, and science fiction.

He does not see himself as perfect by any stretch of the imagination, but rather being perfected each day by Christ's empowerment, love and grace.

About the Book

How did this story get its origin? On one of my better days when moved out of recovery in 2012, after my first heart surgery, I felt compelled to write about my experiences for posterity. It was a strong impression at the time, much like what I felt that time when I took a leap of faith to enter pastoral ministry training.

Since then, I began recording information that came to me; reviewed information recorded in my journals and diaries, spoke with family members and friends with whom I kept in touch over the years. What we have before us is the completed work.

Welcome to my story! It is a tale of the challenges that I faced and how the grace of God and power of prayer enabled me to adapt, change, and accept the will of God over time. This story has three purposes.

First, it emphasizes what I believe to be God's power and wisdom working through my life. This will become obvious to the keen reader through the many examples expressed. Contrary to popular belief that the time of miracle is past, I believe that my life to this point is a miracle of God's saving power and grace.

Second, God does work in our lives through others. No one is an island unto self, as the saying goes. Some may have a vital personal relationship with Him, others may not; but that does not stop the God of the Universe from influencing them to be His hand of aid to others. God is sovereign over His Universe and no one is outside of His purpose and will. This story illustrates the many persons who gave of their time, thought, assistance, and resources, to enable the miracle of God.

Third, this is to give recognition, appreciation and thanks to all who have provided through words of encouragement and hope; lent a hand of help or in any other way assisted me through this journey. As you have done it to me, you have also done it unto Him, the Great Miracle Worker. A miracle indeed!

Book Reviewed

By D.Millin (PhD. Can)
St. Thomas, USVI.

Years of Challenge and Change: An Autobiography is not just inspirational, but tells a human story of the everyday struggles of a Caribbean life on a small island. It chronicles a true life story of love, family and sickness all fortified with hope and resilience; the strength of prayer, and the eventual understanding and acknowledgement of the interdependency of spirituality and practicality of our humanness.

Answorth has used language beautifully, mixing the local Caribbean culture into the most exciting and emotional story of a young boy with a debilitating illness growing up in an environment where basic resources to keep him alive was limited. Yet he takes us through his journey allowing us to experience his hopes, fears, accomplishments, and most of all, coming to the realization that God provides what we need, not necessarily what we think we want.

The story speaks to hope and resilience, underpinned by determination not only by Answorth himself, but his immediate family and friends who he notes provided the love, understanding and caring environment within which he was able to thrive. He provides an insight of not only his struggles with the disease but he takes us on his adventures across islands and continents, in his pursuit of education and professional aspirations. His journey is filled with twists and turns, each with a new hope of healing and wellness, but with each turn God provided the necessary tools and safeguards to achieve another victory. He shows us that even with limitations; it is still possible to achieve what would otherwise seem impossible.

This is a refreshing, inspirational and enlightening story "a must read."

Dedications

All thanks and praise is wholeheartedly given to the Holy One, the Mighty God, blessed be He, for prolonging my days. In honor of His grace, loving kindness and tender mercies, this volume is dedicated. I have experienced the Hand of God moving in my life at every stage of development and His guiding Spirit influencing major decisions.

This is also for Janice, my dearest beloved wife; companion, soul-mate, and supporter in all my adventures for the past forty-one years of married life. For her tender care in times of sickness and hospitalization; her joyous spirit in our times of difficulty; her contentment in our times of need; reminding me often of Paul's admonition in Philippians 4:11 (NRSV), *"Be content with such things as you have,"* and for her encouragement and support in getting this project to the finish line. This is dedicated to you.

To the memory of my mother Bernice Naomi Stevens who nurtured me in sickness and in health; guided me in my formative years on the path of right; and who gave me hope and encouragement when I felt like giving up. For all your loving kindness, this is dedicated.

To my sisters who played a mother's role when I was growing up, especially Elvira, and Margolyn who cared for us when Mom was at work. For Julienne and Daisymae who corrected some of my confusion of information from our youth and for editing the text, thank you.

This book comes to you the general public with the hope of God's blessing. It is my hope that it will inspire you to act as He leads to new opportunities.

Introduction

All things begin in time. Time and space began in God's determination which enables all other things to have their beginning at just the right time. All things depend on time and space for their existence. The existence of the Giant Sequoia tree or the blob fish swimming at the bottom of the ocean off Australia, or the sparrow that freely lives its life in the air, all have their beginning in time. The same is true for all human life including mine. My life began when the time was just right on God's calendar.

Welcome to my story. I came into the world sixty-six years ago at the time of writing. I am the seventh of ten children born to my mother and the twelfth of my father's sixteen children. My father was not consistently in my life as a child. He was what I still call, *"a come-and-go Dad,"* meaning that he did not live with us, he lived by himself and when he wanted to see us he came by. Probably his absence was not unique for the historic period in which I grew up; since it was common practice among many West Indian families to have dads like mine. Now that I have lived through many years and I'm able to reflect on the emotional, sociological, and even psychological drawbacks of such a family structure, I ask myself, "Is there a better way?" Psychologists, Sociologists, and Moralists think there is; and I am partial to their view. It has influenced me to place priority and focus in preaching, teaching and counseling; whenever the opportunity offers itself, to promote and recommend that fathers' be present in the lives of their children on a permanent basis.

Children flourish and are nurtured effectively through the presence, protection and guidance of fathers. As the saying goes, *"Two are better than one,"* (Ecclesiastes 4: 9- 12 NKJV). The context of the passage is not really family life but points to the reasonableness of support under economic and social circumstances. It is therefore needful for fathers and mothers to take this under great consideration if they are going to invest in rearing wholesome children and not just abandon their familial responsibilities.

Rearing a family is hard work under normal two parent supervision. It is probably four times harder for a single parent.

So, I grew up in a single parent household without the consistent influence of my Dad. My Mom endeavored to instill in us high goals and moral values. She labored hard to keep us on the straight and narrow way always instructing and cajoling when we became self-willed and bent towards rebelliousness.

Having been born just at the right time, I also was born with a health challenge. I came into life with a debilitating illness that kept me from doing most things that children did as they matured. The illness limited my physical, social and educational timely advancement but could not deter my aspiration for life.

My Mom and Dad were told that the illness had the potential for death at an early age. This I learned as I became older and could understand the special care given to me above and beyond my siblings. At the age of four years, through the auspices of my Dad's connections and likability by the management the Antigua Sugar Factory, I was fortunate to be one of the first West Indians to benefit from pioneering surgery at the newly opened University Hospital, Kingston, Jamaica.

Though I do not recall all the details and names of all the individuals that had a part in this process, I take this opportunity to thank them and their descendants for what they contributed in making me the person I am today.

All through my life, I have sensed the influence of God's Spirit working through individuals who have contributed to my journey of sixty-six years. What unfolds in the following pages is the story of my journey through those years as best as memory allows.

This is not just my story, it is the weaving of several other peoples' story as those lives touched, influenced, and in some small or large way impacted mine. There is no desire on my part to embarrass, degrade, defame, or derogate, anyone's character, or invade anyone's privacy, thus, actual names, institutions, and places will be freely used to make connections with real people who knew me and contributed in some small or significant way to my experiences over the years.

There are many millions of people who do not give a second thought to their existence since they are blessed or gifted with good health and fortune. But for other hundreds of thousands of us, health concerns are constant reminders that our lives are gifts from a caring God. Those of us who are challenged with health concerns sometimes question ourselves and God as to: *"Why must we struggle for survival?"* Depending on whom you ask, the typical response is: *"Physical suffering is as a result of sin in human life."* This is generally the Judeo-Christian understanding from the viewpoint of the "Fall of Man" in the Garden of Eden, as told by Genesis 3: 1-19 NIV. But within this viewpoint, there is a minority view in the Jewish faith that suggests another cause.

The ancient Rabbis of Israel seem to think that suffering comes from the hand of God to children who must suffer as atonement for the unrighteousness of a community. Abraham Cohen *Everyman's Talmud: The Major Teachings of the Rabbinic Sages* (2008) puts it this way: *"Occasionally, we find it stated that the good suffer on behalf of the bad; e.g. 'When there are righteous in a generation, the righteous are punished for the sins of that generation. If there are no righteous, then the schoolchildren suffer for the evil of the time,'"* (Shab33b - 2008: 125)[1].

There is no definitive answer that will satisfy everyone's concern as to why the individual suffers. In many cases, heredity and or genes malfunction play a vital part in transmitting from

---

[1] The author looks at the corpus of rabbinic literature on the common held view of suffering. The Rabbis seem to think that suffering is not specifically punishment for one's sins or evil. They denied that sufferings endured in this life were intended by God as punishment or that they were evidence of God's disapproval. "On the contrary, they were indicative of his love and served a beneficent purpose," *Everyman's Talmud: The Major Teachings of the Rabbinic Sages* (2008: 125-127). St. John records a story of a man born blind (John 9: 2-3 NKJV) to which the disciples ask Jesus: "Rabbi, Who did sin, this man or his parents why he was born blind?" Jesus' answer clearly points to a reason that they were not willing at the time to accept – that is, "Neither this man nor his parents sinned, but that the work of God should be revealed in him."

one generation to another certain cell defects. In my case, one gene responsible for making red blood cells is defective. The defect causes the blood cells to be immature without full capability of carrying enough oxygen for a healthy lifestyle.

It is my hope that this volume will be both educational and inspirational for many, especially the young who have a health issue or are struggling in the grip of some debilitating illness. It is my hope that this volume also serves the Christian community in building faith in Christ who performs miracles on a daily basis by giving wisdom and understanding in managing one's disability.

Like many sufferers, I have prayed that the illness be taken away just as Jesus took away the blindness of the man born blind in the Gospel of John (9: 1-4 NKJV). As I grew older, I gradually understood that Christ gives us the grace to live with infirmities as an expression of His divine will and purpose in our lives.

Rationally, this is again not my story nor is it that of others whom God placed alongside me during the many years of growth and challenge, but it is about the power and wisdom of God. It is the story of the invisible Hand of God guiding a life during illness and the consequences of poor health. Though

I did not know it at the time, looking back, I have drawn strength from the word of God which many times was the only source of power.

I believe in prayer and over the years, though I may not have gotten what I asked for due to my limited understanding, God answered with what was right for that season of my life.

So, with the lyrics of the songwriter Albert Goodson (1965), I can say that, *"I've come this far by Faith, leaning on the Lord."* Without His power, protection, wisdom and guidance, I would not have had a story to tell.

I believe that what God has done for me, He is well able to do for others in a greater and grander style. Place your life and hope in the hands of the Creator, trust in Him each day to see you through the pain and frustration that are inevitable. In doing this, you will find enough strength to carry on.

Philosophically, life is about choice that brings about challenge, and challenge leads to change. If there is no choice, there can be no challenge and without challenge there can be no change. For example, in life, the choice is literally between life and death. Some will choose death because for them, the challenge of life is too great and complex.

Choosing death is easy – a cop out. Choosing life is a challenge, a fight, a war for survival, and through this battle, comes change of ideas, change of motives, change of actions, change of moral compass, change of direction. I have proven this to be so during my sixty-six years of living, hence, the title. Further, physical and moral life is vitally important but not as important as spiritual life. Paul puts it this way in Ephesians 6:12 (NRSV): *"For our struggle is not against enemies of blood and flesh, but against the rulers, against the authorities, against the cosmic powers of this present darkness, against the spiritual forces of evil in the heavenly places."* We therefore must not only fight for survival in this temporal life but even more so for life eternal.

This story is presented in seven chapters, one for each decade of my life and consists of what I have prayed for over the years and how I believe God has answered those prayers. There is an awareness in my mind, (and should be in yours) that the Almighty God is not beholden to any human being to grant any petition no matter how urgent or fervent, or even how righteous the petitioner is. What I believe moves God in granting a petitioner's prayer is His own grace, love, mercy and compassion toward the one He so chooses within the limits He sets for Himself.

Chapter One

I PRAYED FOR HEALING AND HE GAVE ME TIME

There is no telling of what a person might become after birth. There are numerous possibilities depending on certain factors such as place of birth; family into which the birth occurs, and the accidents of history. As growth takes place, motivation and personal goals are factors in the direction that the life takes, along with appropriate opportunities that contribute to success or failure.

Therefore, one must have a source of power from which to draw strength and encouragement constantly; that source of power for me is the power of prayer. Jesus made this clear in His teaching to His disciples. People are to pray constantly and consistently, petitioning God to meet the need.

Jesus in his teaching stated it this way, (Luke 18: 1 NRSV) *"Then Jesus told them a parable about their need to pray always and not to lose heart."* In essence, what I gather from this statement is that prayer must become integral to one's life. It must be developed into a habit, a custom. As prayer is made, one must be hopeful that the prayer is heard and that the Lord, to whom it ascends will answer; that is the reason for not fainting.

Jesus went on to illustrate his point with the story of the unjust judge and a widowed woman, Luke 18: 2-7 NRSV. He said, *"In a certain city there was a judge who neither feared God nor had respect for people. ³ In that city there was a widow who kept coming to him and saying, 'Grant me justice against my opponent.' ⁴ For a while he refused; but later he said to himself, 'Though I have no fear of God and no respect for anyone, ⁵ yet because this widow keeps bothering me, I will grant her justice, so that she may not wear me out by continually coming.' ⁶ And the Lord said, "Listen to what the unjust judge says. ⁷ And will not God grant justice to his chosen ones who cry to him day and night? Will he delay long in helping them?"* Another way of illustrating this point of consistency in prayer is the example of God and His chosen people held in Egyptian bondage (Genesis 15: 13; Exodus 3: 7-8 NIV). Moses had inquired why God did nothing for four hundred years in answer to their cries of injustice and slavery. Both the widow and the Hebrews exemplify patience and consistency in their plight until the right time came, and God acted to bring about deliverance. I have learned the valuable lesson of praying constantly and consistently through my lifetime and the patience to wait for God's answer in His time and His way.

On Friday, January 18th, 1952, sometime in the evening, I arrived into this vast and wonderful world weighing less than six pounds. I was birth at home on Kentish Road with the help of the district midwife, Nurse Gardner. I was not prematurely born. I was named Answorth Hervan Mackenzie Moitt by my mother. I am the seventh child of my mother's ten children and the eleventh of my father's sixteen children.

My mother Bernice Naomi Christian-Stevens (we called her Mammy) had five previous children from her first marriage to Mr. James Elton Stevens. When that relationship failed, she had another five children by my father, (we called him Pappy). I am second in line of that five.

I was raised in Kentish Village between the alley of Prince Charles Road and Kentish Road. Our neighbors at that time were Mrs. Cookie; Mrs. Murray, the Jarvis'; the Knights, the Williams'; Monty; Little foot Mary to distinguish her from the other Mary who was a fishmonger.

Then, there was John and Doris - farmers; Mrs. Benjamin; Miss. Alcindor who ran a preschool. We played with the children of these families; grew up together and attended mostly the same schools.

I was told by Mammy that I was christened at the Anglican Cathedral somewhere between three and six months of age.

My father was somewhat like the Old Testament Patriarch Jacob who had children with two wives and their two maids (Genesis 29:10 – 30: 26 NIV). He, being likened to the Patriarch Jacob is in no way an approval or condemnation. It was not unusual for that time in our country's social history for some to have many children. He may have understood that *"Children are a heritage from the Lord; offspring a reward from Him"* (Psalm 127: 3 NIV). Unlike the Patriarch Jacob though, he had not the economic resources to effectively support all his children. Because of this lack of financial support, it was strenuous and exhausting for my Mom to keep up with the demands of five growing and needy children, one needier than the others.

I have tried to fathom my ancestry by asking my older siblings as I grew older and by listening in on conversations whenever such talk came up by my mother. Through these means, I got to understand that my father, the first child of his mother, also grew up in a single parent household. He was followed by twins Albert and Victoria; then Lindbergh, Glen and Rosalyn, with only Rosalyn being alive at this time.

I have no knowledge of my paternal grandfather and can only conjecture that none of my siblings knew him either.

I knew my maternal grandfather and grandmother. His name was John Primos Christian and hers Henrietta. They were from Bolans and had their own plot of land. Again, I am not sure of the birth order of my mother's siblings, but her sisters were Martha and Grace – deceased. Her brothers were Clem- the carpenter, Manasseh-the fisherman, Matthew the builder, all passed away, and Noel who went to Santa Domingo to work and never return to Antigua.

My maternal grandfather was short in stature and I guess this was from old age since he walked with a stick for support. He was of very light complexion – almost like a Caucasian with sparse silvery hair. His wife died long before him and my memory of her is faint. She was also of light complexion with long dark hair. They were both always very neatly dressed when they came to visit us from the country.

My mother said that I was a cry-baby. My propensity for crying was probably due in part to the discomfort that I had and would carry every day for the rest of my life. At that time, I had no other way to express the hurt and the pain I felt. I was in a sense what some would call a dependent baby – always requiring the center of attention; which kept my mother from her daily chores.

I came two years after my sister Julienne and after me came Daisymae three years after. Two years after her came our brother Vernon; and two years after him came Kirthon, the last of my father's children by my mother.

Later, as I became fussier, my Mom learned through medical tests that my body was not producing sufficient red blood cells and what was produced were oddly shaped, and the doctors' assessed diagnosis was Sickle-Cell Anemia. Treating the illness required special iron rich diet and she was instructed in my dietary requirements to help alleviate some of my discomfort, and given prescription for medicines that would assist in greater red blood cells production. Due to a low blood count, the consequence was less oxygenation to feed the cells which in turn caused fatigue, tiredness, lethargy and frustration of not being able to participate in strenuous activities.

At age four, my stomach became swollen and near my spleen was quite hard, much like a rock. Each day it would become a little bit more uncomfortable to breath. Again, the doctors told her that the spleen should recycle the broken-down red blood cells back into the system; in this case, there is a malfunction. It had become overwhelmed and so the cells stayed there causing the stiffness in the abdomen. It was the opinion of the physicians also, that unless I could have surgery to remove the spleen, I would die within a few weeks. They counseled that surgery was a difficult procedure which could not be done in Antigua. They also shared the idea that even with success of the surgery; the possibility existed for a shorter life span due to other complications developing post-surgery.

I guess that this information was relayed to my Dad. He was employed by Mr. Alexander Moody-Stewart, the British overseer at the Antigua Sugar Factory. My older brother Harold shared with me that our Dad had a very close relationship with Mr. Stewart due in part to Dad's ability and complexion. My Dad was a painter by profession and he was good at what he did. He seemingly explained to his boss my situation and his lack of resources to do much about it.

It happened that Mr. Stewart knew of a doctor coming out of England on his way to the University Hospital in

Kingston, Jamaica. Through that connection, my Mom was told to have me prepared and ready in a few days to be taken with this doctor to the hospital.

I am not sure how long I stayed in the hospital, possibly six months. This timing sounds right since they needed to evaluate the potential for complications post- surgery. What I do remember is the great number of toys I received while there. The benefits were not only to me but also for the hospital and staff that participated in saving my life. With the success of the surgery, I returned home minus my spleen and a large painful stomach.

I did not start school at five years when most children do because of my illness. It was probably around my seventh year when I started at Miss. Alcindor's pre- school. Miss Alcindor was a short light complexioned stocky Christian lady who ran her preschool out of her front room. She had a large back yard and on sunny days' school was held outdoors. The school was not very far from where we lived, and I remember going there with my sister Daisymae who was three years younger than I. From this preschool, at around eight years old, I attended the Green Bay Primary School for a while. The headmaster was Mr. Henry who was a short man in my view and of a dark skin tone.

I could not run or walk fast like the other children. Recess was quite tiring if I exerted too much energy, so I played marbles which required minimum energy output. Even at that early age, I learned how to adapt to my circumstances and live within the limitation of the illness. At this school, biscuit and milk was provided to all pupils at a certain time of the morning each school day. Periodically, powdered sacks of milk were given to each child to take home.

Academically, I did not do well during these first years of schooling either. First, I started school late and it was difficult for me to catch up with the pace of instruction. Second, I was out of school regularly when hospitalized for weeks at a time. Third, processing information time was delayed, making me somewhat of a borderline slow learner. For these reasons, I did not understand many of the fundamentals of language and math to impact advanced work.

Later in life, I came to recognize that the principle of primary education was scaffolding which means building on former knowledge from one level to the next. If the foundation was weak, then the scaffolding process was also incapacitated. This would affect me all through my school years.

At age eight, I may have been the oldest child in Junior 2 or second grade at Green Bay School. Yet, I paid attention trying to figure out stuff that made no sense. Why it is that one-plus-one equals two? Why one-plus-zero is still one? So I had all this confusion going on in my head and I could not express it clearly for anyone to understand due in part to lack of language skills. I did not know or was not fully aware at the time that this was all due to the illness that I came into the world with.

There was nothing that I or anyone else could do to help my learning experience. Seemingly, the technology was not available in Antigua at the time when I was growing up to have bone marrow transplant or even blood transfusion to make the learning process easier. I guess that the general medical consensus was imminent death at an early age, therefore not much was done.

It was around this time as well that our Mom got an opportunity to go to England. I believe the idea was for her to get us all there eventually. She partially realized that hope by getting two of my older siblings Margolyn and St. Claire to England.

During her absence, we were all taken out of school and sent to live with our paternal grandmother, Ina Looby, in Liberta Village. Her home had room only for one bed and we slept on mats on the floor huddled close together.

Our grandmother was a short, plump, woman with long beautiful black hair and our father had most of her facial structure and features.

Grandma lived on a hill surrounded by a sugar cane plantation on the left and a fruit and vegetable plantation on the right of her property belonging to an owner called Banny. She grew her own fruits and vegetables on her plot that spanned a greater distance up the hill.

Living in the country was somewhat an exciting experience. We were registered in the (Ball-beaf) village school where Mr. Roberts was Principal. He too was not very tall in my eyes and he had a propensity to discipline with the belt even for getting to school late.

We enjoyed the fresh breezes and wide open land spaces. We also had the freedom to roam during school vacations going down to places like Cobb's Cross and English Harbor without adult supervision.

When school was not out on vacation, the drawback for us was, we had to fetch cooking firewood on Fridays' up Bailey's hill. The Bailey's were family friends of grandma and they would give us honey from their hives to take home, fruits that were in season, and tamarind that we would eventually shell and take to the city to be sold for soap making. At the time, it was fun and I did not see that there would have been further long term consequences.

Our grandmother was a Seventh - day Adventist and all cooking had to be finished by Friday afternoon before sunset. This was her reason for taking us out of school each Friday for two years so that all things would be in place for Sabbath worship.

In summary, my first ten years of life was filled with pain, adaptations and adjustments to my environment, as well as with joy and hope for future relief. From the time I could talk, my Mom began teaching me to pray and ask the Lord for help. Our grandmother emphasized it as well for us to take our concerns to the Lord. So, before we went to sleep, I asked the Lord to heal me. I prayed for healing and He, in wisdom, gave me time. My Evening and Morning Prayer at this stage of life went something like this:

"Lord, I need your healing now to make my life as normal as possible. Thank You for medicines that are helping in this. Let Your will be done in me through your Son, Jesus Christ. Amen."

As I became more self-aware, gradually I began formulating in my mind ways of making other lives less stressful and mine more independent and self-reliant.

Chapter Two

PRAYED FOR HEALING AND HE GAVE ME AN EDUCATION

"Life happens!" Not always as it is planned but contrary to our best intentions, it happens. We must be flexible to adjust when life encounters a detour or some obstruction in order to survive. Maybe Paul's experience can be instructive at this point. (Acts 16:5-7 NRSV) we read, *"So the churches were strengthened in the faith and grew daily in numbers. After the Holy Spirit prevented them from speaking the word in the province of Asia, they travelled through the regions of Phrygia and Galatia they came to the border of Mysia, they tried to enter Bithynia, but the Spirit of Jesus would not permit them."* What we sometimes think is a set back or hindrance to our desired progress is not always so, according to God's design. In this instance, the gospel of Christ converted Lydia and her household in Philippi, thus starting a new fellowship.

In the previous chapter I mentioned that my Mom went to England with the intent of having us join her there. What made her return to Antigua before her plans were realized?

Reasons for her returning, I can only surmise that she may have found life there more difficult than she had thought. Maybe she was unhappy; or, maybe our grandmother wrote to her and gave a bad report on our behavior. Possibly the winter months were unbearable for her. She mentioned several times on her return that there were moments in England that she could not eat well due in part to not knowing how we were faring.

I was happy for her being back home. We returned to Kentish Village on her arrival and were reunited as a single parent family. In those early years of her return, we had no running water or electricity. Gradually, these amenities would be added.

My mother worked hard to maintain the family. She took in other people's laundry as a part-time washer-woman. She went out to work as a house servant with the Michaels on Market Street and later on High Street in the city, six days per week. She would leave for work after seeing us off to school for 9 o'clock and would return sometimes at 5 o'clock in the evening.

We were registered in Ottos School where Mr. Maynard, a lanky, fair complexioned man, was Principal. I believe that I was placed in junior four or fourth grade. From

Ottos school, we were transferred to Golden Grove School within a year where Mr. Quinn, a minister/pastor of Pilgrim Holiness Church; tall and gaunt; was the first Principal; and he was replaced by Mr. Samuels; a man of medium height and weight but very good-humored.

In fifth grade or junior five, my teacher at Golden Grove School was Mrs. Mary Quinn, wife of the Principal I was not given an opportunity to take the primary school exam due to my advanced years for the class. This exam was taken by pupils at age eleven plus, whereby if they passed, they received from the government a five-year scholarship to a secondary education.

I remained at Golden Grove School and took the post-primary exam in senior three or eighth grade and passed for a two-year scholarship at the Princess Margaret Secondary School.

We went back to the Anglican Cathedral for worship services. When I was around twelve, my sister Daisymae and I were confirmed. A few months later, I became an altar boy or server. When my other two younger brothers Vernon and Kirthon were confirmed a year or so later, I was able to incorporate them as altar boys as well. Our responsibility as altar boys were not limited to the services on Sundays but we were required to serve on a rotation basis at the six o'clock AM mass during the week as well. This meant that we had to leave home around five AM to walk the miles or so to get to the church from where we lived on Kentish Road.

From a theological perspective, the repetition of certain aspects of the Mass such as the Nicene Creed in almost all the services was of great help for me along with the 23rd psalm and the Lord's Prayer. Also, celebration of the Eucharist at each service was for me a source of grace, renewal and healing.

When I was not waking up early to go to church, I woke up early to carry Miss Celestine's bread basket from the bakery on Kentish Road to several shops in the city. Just as how many American boys in that time period would have a paper route delivering the daily newspaper, many of them on bikes; I had a bread route as a bread boy but without the bicycle. The bakery was in the village, a short distance from our home. Bakers would bake their wares between two and three o'clock in the morning six days per week. Delivery boys would get to the bakery for five o'clock to distribute the wares. The wicker baskets were packed in order of first to last delivery which was carried on the head by each delivery boy. Delivery boys had to remember each shop's order so that no mistake is made. For this routine, I receive one dollar per week and a loaf of bread for each day. No one educated me then that I was a child laborer and I was taken advantage of. For me, it was an experience in learning the layout of the city, learning how small businesses operate and a lesson in self-sufficiency.

I graduated from bread-boy to errand boy, passing my bread route on to my brother Vernon. There was an American woman by the name of Mrs. Williams who had a vanity store on Kentish Road, adjacent to Mr. Kenneth Richardson's grocery store. She was on island about half of the year, when the American summer ended. She took an interest in me and asked my Mom if I could be allowed to do chores for her. So, I went to her home and did chores after school. I was asked to clean the windows and furniture; wash dishes, clean fish, run errands and purchase groceries. After some months when her brother went back to the USA, I started sleeping over in her home to keep her company. I would leave early in the morning to prepare for school. She paid for me to learn typing at Mrs. Henry's Typing School in Gambols Terrace for one year.

The largest grocery store in the village was run by Mr. Kenneth and his wife Gwendolyn Richardson. I do not remember how the connection was made for me to be serviceable to them, but I started doing shop preparation early in the morning for them as well. This was after Mrs. Williams did not return to the island for a long while.

I was required to reach the store at five o'clock each morning. I was responsible for sweeping up both the back and front of the store as well as inside. Once that was done, my next task was to mix and bottle vinegar – three parts water to one-part vinegar. Essence was a different combination one vial to four vials of water. Cooking oil came in fifty-five-gallon drums and had to be measured out into twenty-six ounce bottles and pint size bottles. Next came the weighing of sugar, rice, flour, corn meal into one- pound packages; which had to be stacked in their place for the shop's opening at eight o'clock. Second-to-last chore was the washing of the car and my final chore was to go upstairs and clean the breakfast dishes and tidy the kitchen before leaving at around eight-thirty to prepare for school. After a while, I was asked to return after school to help in the shop itself. Again, I was rewarded with two dollars each week for my services.

All of the above experiences assisted me in learning a little better because they were practical application of math and oral language communication skills. The drawback for me many times was reaching school late and not being focus and attentive in class. I was disciplined several times for being tardy. Once, Mr. Samuels lined up all the late comers and before beating us, said for us to repeat, *"Punctuality is the soul of business."* Since that day, I've made punctuality one of my character traits.

At Golden Grove School, there were three teachers that positively impacted my learning. They challenged me with my limitations. Mrs. Quinn was the first to recognize that I had ability if the instruction was given in a manner that allowed me to work at a slower pace.

She gave me a choice; take recess or stay during recess to go over what I did not fully understand. I chose the latter. She took the time to help me go over critical information shared during the class and gave me opportunity to rework what I did incorrectly. She instilled in me the wonders of reading and explained to me that books open the imagination to different worlds. It was almost compulsory for all her students to take a book each week from the mobile library. At that time, one teacher taught all the subjects so they got to know the students' strengths and weaknesses. I remember I wrote a poem in her class that she thought was outstanding, and entered me in a competition held island-wide for the grade. I was placed third in that competition held at the Boys School.

When I move up from her class to senior 2 or seventh grade, Mrs. Alice Henry-Buckley was my teacher. She also was a fine teacher who placed priority on making sure I understood the lessons. She challenged us to put in more effort at home in reading and math practice in order to be prepared for success. She was interested in all her students' success as well. I had difficulty understanding geometry and algebra, but made the minimum grade to pass the class.

Mrs. Hilda Richards was my final teacher at Golden Grove School. She prepared the students who were identified as candidates to take the Post Primary Exam. The assessment focused on written English essay, history of the Caribbean, math (arithmetic, algebra and geometry), health science, social studies and geography. The exam was late May or early June just before the closing of school for the summer holidays.

I was seventeen years when I took the exam. About twelve students from my school took the test and five passed (Janice Brown, Pamela Cainns, Hezekiah Lewis, Glanville Gordon, and me). Those who did not take the test and those who took it and did not pass had no other choice but to leave school. They received a school leaving certificate to access jobs.

From senior three to fourth form at Princess Margaret Secondary School where Mr. Basil Peters was Principal; was for me a great leap academically and financially. In all my previous schools the teachers taught from the texts by writing the information on chalkboard and students would copy in their exercise books. Students did not have the texts. In high school, parents were given a materials and text books list for purchasing same. For example, math required three different texts (algebra, geometry, arithmetic). Science required two texts, English literature two texts, and I was placed in woodwork course that required two texts.

The fourth form I was placed in consisted of thirty-two students from all parts of the island. The teachers came for their class period of seventy-five minutes and taught their subjects. Ms. Evelyn Davis taught math and was good at it. In my view, she taught at an amazingly quick pace. In my reflection, only a few brilliant students were able to keep up with her and correctly answer questions in open discussion.

Mr. Alexander taught woodwork and students went to the woodwork shop for both theory and practice. Miss. Patsy Barker taught religious studies and history; for religious studies we studied the book of Acts of the Apostles. Mrs. Simon taught health science and I don't remember at this time who taught

English Literature, but I remember we did Shakespeare's *Romeo & Juliette* the first year and *Merchant of Venice* the second year.

In fourth form, I made new friends. Caleb Benjamin and Patrick Samuels became my buddies since we were living in the same general area of each other. We would read western novels by Louis Lamour and go to the Public Library to read for pleasure; and once in a while to the movies. I stated taking an interest in Janice Brown, she lived off Christian Street and we would meet up and walk to and from school on a regular basis.

I liked wood work and I would go to the shop if I had a free period or a cancelled class. I developed a relationship with Mr. Alexander and he made me one of his assistants. I would assist him in sanding cabinets and gluing parts for furniture. Later, he would take me with him on his installation jobs. He also organized for me to do odd jobs on weekends. For example, one summer, he took me to a home to work on a floor at one of his colleague's residence. The house had a wooden floor in bad condition and had to be refurbished. First, I had to scrub off all the debris, putty the creases and holes, sand down the rough areas, apply linseed oil, leave for a few days before applying several top coats of varnish.

In fifth form, students had to determine what subjects they would write at the General Certificate of Education (GCE) ordinary level. Students who got a two-year scholarship sat the London GCE while students who had the five-year scholarship sat the Cambridge GCE, where five subjects were the minimum to take. I did the London exam in four subjects (English, English Literature, Religious Studies and West Indian history) and passed only the history. I finished school at nineteen years of age.

On leaving school, I worked with Charles Shoul in his auto parts shop on Newgate Street during the summer of 1971. Part of my job was to make vehicle registration plates. The process was quite simple. The plates came in standard black rectangle aluminum, approximately ten inches long by three inches wide. When the number was issued to the owner of the vehicle, they presented it to the clerk at the store and the clerk would pass the information to me in the back. I would select the white plastic letters and numbers, place them on the plate, mark the place where the holes will be punched, punch out the holes with a mechanical machine, then squeeze in the letters and numbers making them secure. Sometime later, the numbers and letters came in pre-glued backing so that I would just remove the peel-off portion and stick them onto the plate.

Another aspect of my job was to sort and store the vehicular parts when they came into the store from Customs. This was a bit more technical because they were to be stacked according to vehicle type and part numbers. For the few months I worked there I enjoyed the experience since it brought me in contact with cars and the people who owned them. It was there that I first sat in the driver's seat and started a car.

In September of 1971, I began making applications to find a real job. Many applications were sent out and I determined at that time that the first company who offered, I would accept. My first job was at Antigua Printing and Publishing Company with the Times Newspaper. Mrs. Bridget Harris interviewed me for the job and outlined my responsibilities as a photographer/reporter. It was there I met the famous Gerald Price one of the island's best-known photographers. He taught me how to use the camera, how to develop and fix the negative, how to print the pictures. So, I would report to work at eight o'clock in the morning and finish at five o'clock in the evening with the understanding that news always happens, and I must be ready to go at any moment. I would interview people and take pictures; get from the Police Department or the Court any bulletins for public notice. Sometimes story and picture were good enough to be published. My typing skills were put to good use since I had to take notes in the field and then rewrite the story on the typewriter. One piece that was published was a yacht that caught fire in English Harbor, November of 1971. For my efforts, I was compensated twenty-five dollars per week.

Mr. Alfred Lewis was a friend of the family. He was a Civil Servant and band master of the Salvation Army Band; he was able to give me a written recommendation. Sometime in October of 1971, I was called to an interview at the Establishment Department to join the Civil Service. The message came via Mr. Lewis. I had the interview and on leaving I thought I did poorly since I sat around a table with seven or nine distinguished looking men and women. They fired questions to which I was not sure I gave adequate answers. After about ten minutes, I was told that I would hear from them if I was selected.

Weeks passed and then, one Monday afternoon after Christmas, Mr. Lewis came by and told me that I was selected to go for training to join the service. The training was for three months (Monday through Friday) without pay at the University Center on Factory Road. I gave up the newspaper job to attend. I made it each day and on time. At the close of the course, Mr. Flax, one of the instructors told us that there were no guarantees that all of us would be hired; we would be contacted as openings became available.

In mid-March of 1972, amidst all the turmoil of politics and change of government, I was called via Mr. Lewis to report to the Treasury Department of the Ministry of Finance to start as a Clerical Assistant. There, for an entire year, I checked pay sheets submitted by three ministries: The Ministry of Education, Ministry of Agriculture, and the Ministry of Health. My job also included checking and delivering warrants (the document submitted to the treasury from the Magistrate Court on behalf of mothers to collect child support) and delivering them to the recipients. My first month's salary was fifty percent more than the previous job with the newspaper.

It was not particularly easy for me to achieve the grand old age of twenty. I had numerous and painful critical periods, frequent hospitalizations, several clinic and doctor visits, and more infusions of dextrose and saline than I can remember. I was not a complainer nor did I become angry and bitter with myself or make the condition rule over my mental acuity. I did not blame anyone but rather tried to understand and live within my physical limitations. I believe at that time that my faith and religious practice would be seen by the Almighty as an offering, which He would soon recompense in a miraculous healing.

Mom instilled in us the maxim, *"Do good and good will follow you wherever you go."* And I thought that by this time I would see good health that would make my life normal as everyone else's. I prayed every day for this and I lived in a heightened mental state of expectancy for the desired outcome of my faith:

> *"Lord God, creator of all that is, You have given me life for which I am thankful. You have done great things for others by healing them and answering their prayers. Hear my prayers today and take away the discomfort and disease. I want Your will to be fulfilled in my life and so I thank you for what You have done and what you are yet to do. Amen."*

I prayed more earnestly for healing, but He gave me in his wisdom an education. I was open to the new educational opportunities that came my way and made great effort to utilize it effectively.

Temperamentally, I was passive in nature but patient with myself and others.

Chapter Three

I PRAYED FOR HEALING AND HE GAVE ME A WIFE

Life continues! Without achieving my desired miracle of transformation, I continued to do the best I could while keeping expectation alive. I expected that the God of miracles, blessed be He, would bring about complete healing at any moment, because I wanted to share that with others for Christ's glory. The words of Jesus that heightened my expectation of a healing miracle are these: *"Therefore I say unto you, what things soever you desire, when you pray, believe that you receive them, and you shall have them,"* (Mark 11:24KJV). Jesus again gives reason for granting a petitioner's request: *"Whatever you ask in My name, that will I do, so that the Father may be glorified in the Son,"* (John 14: 13 KJV). Therefore I lived in that sphere of expectation that the request for restoration of improved health would be granted, and life would become healthier and happier for the rest of my days.

In 1973, I was transferred from the Treasury Department to the Customs Department, Ministry of Finance main office, situated at the bottom of St. Mary's Street; where Mr. Norman Abbott was Comptroller of Customs. Part of my job as a junior officer was to check import and export documents to make sure the correct duties and taxes were applied to each item. The process required knowing the different categories and sub-categories for imported items particularly, in order to calculate the correct import duties and taxes. Some items for example required the payment of duty but were tax exempt. Another category for instance was printed books that were only taxable but free of import duty. One became proficient at this by patience, practice and repetition.

It was necessary to work at a fast pace since there were other factors to consider. First, when cargo arrived via ship, the Port Authority warehousing rule allowed a ten-day free storage; after which, a fine was charged for each additional day. Second, if the warrant was inaccurately calculated by the Custom Broker, on presentation of the document to Customs, a re-write in some cases had to be made after it was corrected by Customs. Third, if there were an item incorrectly classified, a physical check had to be made and verified by an onsite officer at the cargo shed.

Later, I was trained to operate the cash register in order to substitute in the absence of the cashier. Knowledge is power, and so, almost all the officers in the department knew how to manipulate the machine accurately. At the close of the day, a supervisor would check the tape from the machine and the documents to verify the day's taking; while another senior officer would check the money. All three must synchronize before the cashier is allowed to leave.

I started thinking about owning a piece of land. I made an application to the ministry responsible for Housing and Urban Development to acquire the same. Promises were made but never kept. In conversation on the matter with Mr. Roy Constant, he told me he had a house plot he wanted to sell, and if I was interested, he would show it at my convenience. We settled on a day to see it. The corner lot in Skerritts Pasture measured 50'x100' and was priced at three thousand five hundred dollars and we settled for three thousand.

For the purchase, I had to take a loan from Scotia Bank to establish my credit worthiness. My repayment was around a hundred dollars per month for three years.

Sometime in 1974, I was transferred to the Airport Cargo Division of Customs. My supervisor was Mrs. Idabelle Matthias, now deceased. My duty was manifest clerk reconciling all the documents for each shipment that came by air. Every three months or so, merchandise that remained unclaimed were put up for sale by auction.

From manifest clerk, I was trained by Mr. Leebert Skepple and John Irish to carry out physical examination of imported items that came without invoices. Personal items were the easiest to deal with. Again, knowing the custom manual was a necessity for effectively doing this. During slow periods of the day, I would go through the manual to enhance my understanding. Sometimes, I was given overtime to receive cargo when the office was closed at four o'clock. This enhanced my earnings quite a bit.

Around July of 1975, Mr. Heskett Phillip and I were selected and sent to the Customs Training Unit, Port of Spain, Trinidad, on a six months' course. On our first day, we were introduced to the rest of the class consisting of the Trinidad contingent of fourteen officers; two from Tortola, British Virgin Island; two from Turks and Caicos Islands, two Bermudans, two St. Lucians, two Bahamians, one Anguillan, one Grenadian, and one Montserratian; making a class of twenty-nine officers.

Instruction and practice centered on Custom Laws and Procedures including Carifta Agreement, Excise Laws and Procedures; Purchase Tax Laws and Procedures; Laws and Procedures governing Approved and Assisted Industries; Agency Duties, and Human Relations. We were paid our usual salaries by our various governments back home and awarded through the sponsors of the program six hundred TT dollars per month for expenses.

Heskett and I stayed with Mrs. Walker in Cocorite, near Diego Martin, for the duration of our stay. Two other students who started out there moved out within a week of the course. I found her rate of ten dollars per day reasonable for board and lodge since it included breakfast, a sack lunch, and full dinner.

A typical day started around six AM. Breakfast was at six-thirty and our ride to the center came for seven. Class started at eight and each succeeding class ran for an hour with a fifteen minutes break around ten, with-a-half-hour lunch break at twelve. Our afternoon sessions ended at three and sometimes when the traffic was good we would get home by four o'clock. Dinner was at five-thirty and we would do our homework assignments until around ten o'clock.

I liked best the practical aspect of the course. The field days were exciting as we visited industrial parks and talked with the officers who monitored and implemented the import and export laws and regulations; the visits to the distilleries and breweries to observe the process and the implementation of the rules and regulations governing the process.

At the end of the course, we had two exams, one oral the other written over a two-day period. In the oral portion, the five instructors who ran the course asked two questions each. The written portion was essay questions; some with three or four situational problems; for which extensive answers were required. When the results were published, I did very well graduating with honors. For the duration of my stay, I did not get sick nor had a health crisis.

I returned home at the end of the course with about nine-hundred TT dollars which had an exchange rate of one dollar twelve cents in Eastern Caribbean Currency. I was able to clear my debt at the bank with that money.

Meanwhile, Janice was in the nurses' training program at the Holberton Hospital. After leaving school, our relationship gradually became somewhat serious and we determined to continue seeing each other. She was short- around five feet two inches; dark complexion, short kinky hair and possibly weighing the same as me.

She is the second or middle child of her mother Gwendolyn Richardson's three children. She had just about the same upbringing as myself and is resilient, motivated in pursuing her goals, and very wise.

Our relationship continued to develop by seeing each other every day. We would spend time in the evenings when she was off from work and at home. I would visit her and we would sometimes be on a date at the Nook on St. Mary's Street having ice cream. She had an insatiable love for Cadbury chocolate and I took pleasure in meeting the need. At other times when she was at the nurses' hostel, I would see her there and we would take long walks in the evenings just to talk and be in each other's company. With time, we fell in love and had our engagement commitment at my home December 1975 when I returned from Trinidad.

Janice was also a member of the Anglican Church and a Sunday school teacher there. She also was involved in preparing candidates for confirmation.

What was the attraction for me? Janice was for me a beautiful girl that I knew from elementary and high school. She was a person of high moral standard with quiet strength and determination. She was not as tempestuous and daring as some others with whom I shared the same class during high school. Our backgrounds were similar, and as I got to know her better, I felt that we were destined to be together for the rest of our lives. Some may call this natural magnetism. Our love relationship was not a *'love at first sight'* kind of love, but rather one that developed over time as we shared our hopes and aspirations.

She was invited by Hilary James of Zion Church of God – Monroe and Bernice Spencer were pastors – to attend one of their special evening evangelistic services in 1975, while I was in Trinidad. Hilary was also a classmate of ours at PM school who became a dispenser trainee at the Holberton Hospital, the same time she was doing her nursing program. She became a convert some weeks later to evangelicalism.

Her conversion to evangelicalism was a difficult time in our relationship; in that an ultimatum was issued; and I was put on guard that her faith in Christ and a developing personal relationship with Him, meant more than our relationship. This did not stop her from inviting me to visit the church.

Her persistence paid off when one Sunday evening in January '76 I visited the fellowship. I was challenged by the missionary message which had a profound impact on me. It took me a while to start going regularly. On one occasion, I felt the influence of the Holy Spirit drawing me to a personal commitment of my life to Christ. I went and knelt at the altar and prayed the prayer of forgiveness and reception of Christ as my personal Lord and Savior as well as for my healing:

> *"Heavenly Father, You have been my helper over the course of my life to this point. Maybe I have angered You through my disbelief, my unforgiving spirit, my anger, my fear instead of faith. I confess that I am not all that You expect of me. I now confess and repent of my sin and ask Your forgiveness for every offensive thought, deed or action that displeases You. Now Lord, transform this illness into normal health, according to your love, Your grace, Your wisdom and power. I am waiting upon You for this, and in return, I am dedicating myself to Your ministry to do your will, in Jesus Christ. Amen."*

I was baptized in March of that year during a Quarterly Service held on Fort James' beach by Pastor Edmond Green and Pastor Malcolm James (both now deceased).

The five congregations located in – St. John's, Bendals, Bethesda, Sea View Farm, and Freemans Village – shared fellowship during Quarterly Services. It was a special time when candidates are baptized and introduced to the entire body of believers; and services for each quarter would be rotated in order that all members would be acquainted.

I became reacquainted with Bro. Norris Ferris who had lived on Tyndale Road, not very far from our home when we were growing up. At one time, he was the church's bus driver, later became Pastor of Sea View Farm Fellowship, and he was for me, a source of encouragement and inspiration. Bro. Ivor Davis, Everton Michael, Harry Piper, were quite active and influential in the life and ministry of the church. Also active and influential was Sis. Ingrid Phillip, Ursula Martin, Bernadette Roberts, among others that memory fails to bring to remembrance at this point. They were for example, worship leaders, youth leaders and sometimes preachers on Sunday evening services and Youth Sundays. They were the force in planning the annual Youth Camp and Convention. Later, I was integrated into this group.

The church also had a band in which the four sons of Sis. Ethlyn Williams – Royston, Keith, David, and Elton, played, they would interchange between playing the keyboard, guitars and the drums. Prior to that time, Bro. Hilary James and Bro. Oliver Parker were members as well.

I learned a great deal of Bible from Sis. Ethlyn Williams. She was the adult Sunday school teacher during those years. I also gained great insights from the teaching ministry of Pastor Bernice Spencer who taught more than preach the Word.

For me, Pastor Monroe Spencer was, in his ministry of the Word, would stress its practical application for personal Christian development. Both had a profound influence on shaping my faith and later call to ministry. They are now in the presence of their Lord.

As Evangelical Christians, sexual immorality was sin. Abstinence from sex until marriage was a virtue and preached regularly. Looking back, such admonition was required, due in part to the number of teens and youth in the fellowship. There was an active weekly youth program with healthy discussions on various social/moral issues that confronted both the church and the youth.

I took interest in the organizational structure and history of the church; this branch of the body of Christ named Zion *Church of God Reformation* as it differentiated itself from other denominations. Part of my education came through the youth fellowship. I learned that the church was established sometime in 1934 by a Christian native Lady who returned from New York, USA; with certain Christian teachings she acquired in the Reformation Movement. She was influenced by the Reformation Movement out of Indiana, USA started by D. S. Warner. Warner's theology emphasized three particular aspects: holiness of life, unity in polity and Divine healing.

I took driving lessons for about two months in 1976. The first time I took the road test I failed it because I could not get the vehicle to stand still when asked to do so on the hill; the car rolled back a few inches. A month later, I retook the test and passed it. This time I had the use of a newer car lent to me by Mr. Afflack of Market Street.

In July of 1977, my sister Julienne got married to Leslie Williams. Prior to their wedding, Janice and I had already set our wedding date for September 29th of that year. In preparation for our life together, I got a loan from Barclays Bank on High Street; to construct our first home on the lot previously purchased in Skerritts Pasture. Our budget built a two-bedroom home with no kitchen and no bath. When Pastor Bernice Spencer came to bless the home, she promised that she and her husband would bless us with the money to attach the missing rooms. Thus, when we moved in, it was a petite, neat and comfortable owned home without rent. Some furniture were provided by Janice' Aunt Eileen who came from St. Croix, US Virgin Islands, and fitted her out also for the occasion. I prayed for healing and He in wisdom gave me a loving, caring, and beautiful wife.

We were married on September 29th 1977 at the Zion Church of God situated on North Street. Our marriage took place at eight o'clock in the morning. Pastor Edmond Green officiated. My best man was Bro. Griffith James (now deceased) and Bro. Norris Ferris was Janice's father giver. Our reception was at the home of Mr. Clarence Elm's residence with music provided by the band from the church.

We tried casually at first to have a baby in the early months and years of our marriage. Janice's desire was to have half-a-dozen children. We prayed and we asked selected persons to pray with us for this to be realized. We kept appointments with gynecologists and a male health doctors who specializes in reproductive health, and were treated individually for bringing about conception but were unsuccessful. We kept our faith believing that a miracle would happen. We kept on trying month-after-month and year-after-year for three years; our efforts were unsuccessful.

In 1979, I bought our first pre-owned car from Dr. Ramsey, a blue *Datsun*. Although it was second hand and a manual shift, it ran well with little maintenance for the first few years.

Mid 1980, Janice received a call followed by a letter from the Peebles Hospital administration, Tortola, British Virgin Islands, offering her a five-year contract. We had prayed about the decision for a couple of weeks. We discussed the various implications if the offer was to be accepted or rejected. It was impractical at the time for both of us to relocate due in part to the intended living arrangements provided by the hospital, and to our mortgage commitment at home. There was also no guarantee that I would have found immediate employment to keep up the payment on our home. We agreed for her to accept the offer and we would travel back and forth to be with each other.

Janice left for Tortola in the month of October 1981. Her absence was devastating in the sense of me having no one to talk with; no one to return home to after a long day at work; no one to eat with at mealtimes; and no one to share my bed at nights. Our three-and-a-half years of togetherness made a great impact and the suffering of parting was shared mutually.

Pastor Malcolm Phillip (now deceased) returned from his pastoral studies with God's Bible School located in Cincinnati, Ohio, USA, sometime in 1978. The Spencer's were happy for him to take over the reign of leadership in St. John's. Thus, for the next two years, the fellowship continued to grow both numerically and spiritually. Pastor Phillip made it known that he had plans to return to the USA to work with the Clinton Springs Church of God where he had done his internship. Work was in progress for him to migrate with his family there in the not too distant future. His call back to the USA came in 1981; which permitted a leadership meeting of minds to chart the way forward for the five fellowships.

In the reshuffle of ministers, Pastor Price was recommended by Pastor Edmond Green and was assigned to lead the fellowship in Sea View Farm. This took place because the Ferris's who pastured the fellowship got their call also to migrate to St. Thomas, US Virgin Islands. Since Pastor Prince was new to the organization, I volunteered to assist him in ministry tasks, especially on Friday evenings with the Youth Fellowship. We also did visitations in the village in order for him to become better acquainted with the members.

The child for whom we had prayed came to us on this wise. While we were not thinking of adoption, we were made aware by a friend, that a situation came to light for one if we were interested. Again, we made it a matter of prayer and asked God's direction on the matter. Janice had already left for her new job and so we discussed by phone and letter what decision would be best. We would benefit with making the decision to accept the child since he would bring into our lives the joy and hopes of sharing our lives with him. Maybe after his arrival, we would naturally have at least one of our own. The child also would benefit from our care and supervision becoming an integral part of our lives. Such a situation also came with fears and anxieties; but we believed at that time that the Lord would make straight what was crooked (Isaiah 40: 4). And so we did. This was God's doing in answer to our prayer. We named him Charles Pernelle Nathaniel.

Chapter Four

I PRAYED FOR HEALING AND HE GAVE ME A COLLEGE DEGREE

..."*With God, all things are possible*," (Matt. 19: 26b KJV), said Jesus. It was a shocking statement to his disciples; they were in disbelief. The context of the statement is on the things that people love more than God. The rich man wanted to know how to enter into eternal life and asked Jesus what is required (Matt.19: 16-26 KJV). The disciples hearing Jesus' response; seeing the man walking away in reaction; was astounded. They raised the issue: *"Who then can be saved?"* Jesus responds, *"With men, this is impossible, but with God, all things are possible."*

He shared with them the difficulty of the rich person getting into the kingdom. I guess He was saying that rich people can be saved when they focus on the right use of riches rather than personal aggrandizement. The difficulty can be overcome with faith and the right use of wealth. At times, we doubt ourselves as to what we can accomplish. I've heard a variant take of the aphorism attributed to Elbert Green Hubbard

(1856-1915) that said, *"Those who say it can't be done have not the right to critique the one who does it."* I was told repeated times that I was too fragile, too weak, too small in stature, too ill to accomplish anything worthwhile. Nevertheless, with God, all things are possible.

At school, I was called names by others to make me feel less than equal and more inadequate. I was written off by physicians who counseled that I should be kept at home with little activity and wait to die. Their prognosis after my splenectomy was five more years of life. Then gradually they believed I would not reach the age of twenty since other persons who had the same condition died early. In their understanding, this was considered the compassionate outlook, they thought it was in my best interest, and I could not even now fault them for their advice to my parents. Yet, with God, all things are possible. It turned out that I was stronger than thought. I was a fighter because I had a great zest for life and God.

In June of 1982, President Carlton Cumberbatch of West Indies Theological College was in Antigua visiting the churches seeking candidates who felt a call to Pastoral or Christian Education Ministry. I listened intently to his presentation, and asked a few questions about entry requirement. He indicated that four O Levels were required for entering the diploma program. Students who did not have this minimum would be able to work on getting it in the first year of study. My other questions centered on costs. Since I did not have any money, I asked if scholarships were available. He assured me that there was some work on campus that could help to defray some cost. The diploma in pastoral ministry course was three years or ninety-academic hours.

After the meeting, I thought about my best course of action. We now have an adopted child to care for; we have a mortgage; what would happen if I gave up my employment to go away and study? Would study at this juncture be an advantage? Would my health hold up under the pressure of study? This was a challenge.

I did not have the money or the educational qualification to do it. And yet, a still small voice in my head said, *"Go for it. Trust your future in the hands of the Master, who created Universe."* Logically, financially, educationally it did not make sense, but it was as if this was my destiny. Thus, began a new challenge that would change the course of my life.

I found assurance that this was the right course of action in my devotional reading of Proverbs 3: 1-6 NRSV.

"My child, do not forget my teaching, but let your heart keep my commandments; ² for length of days and years of life and abundant welfare they will give you. ³ Do not let loyalty and faithfulness forsake you; bind them round your neck, write them on the tablet of your heart. ⁴ So you will find favor and good repute in the sight of God and of people. ⁵ Trust in the LORD with all your heart, and do not rely on your own insight. ⁶ In all your ways acknowledge him, and he will make straight your paths."

I found an inner calm in the anxious moments after I made the decision to move forward, trusting that this course of action would bring success, and that it would inevitably serve the glory of Christ.

I began saving my overtime money from June through the end of August. I applied for leave without pay for three years, and it was granted. I signed up with the Department of Education to retake the three subjects in English, English Literature and Religious Studies. I ordered the study material out of London and began reading. I also sold my car to my brother Hudson, who at that time worked at the Antigua Catering Services. I put the house up for rent which my sister Julienne would manage for me so that the mortgage was paid in my absence.

In early September of 1982, I purchased my ticket, boarded a British West Indian Airways flight, landed at Piarco International Airport, Trinidad, on a Sunday evening to start my course of study. President Carlton Cumberbatch himself came to collect me. The campus was and still is located outside of San Juan, on La Pastora Road, Upper Santa Cruz.

I joined a class of four other students who started out on the same journey. They were John Small, Loraine Straker, Dianna Burrows - all from Barbados, and Nair Persad from Guyana.

The campus was small but comfortable. I shared a dorm with three other upper classmen; Bro. Phipps from St. Kitts, Bro. Maynard from Barbados, and Bro. Fidel James from Tobago.

On Monday, I did all the registrations for class assignments and with the other students, was oriented to the campus. We also signed up for our work schedules and given time sheets to record hours worked. Assignments of lawn service, metal-workshop, and kitchen duties were rotated each week for a total of ten hours per week per student. It was also the expectation that students would familiarize themselves with the local congregations in order to sharpen their communication and interpersonal skills. Upper classmen and women were mostly working with local fellowships doing actual preaching, teaching, and managing churches as pastors' assistants.

On Tuesday, we were taken to the city to make purchases of needed supplies to start our classes on Wednesday. Classes started at 8:00 AM and ran some days till 2:00 PM. Each class session was ninety minutes with a fifteen-minute break between classes. My schedule was heavier on Monday, Wednesday, and Friday when I did English grammar, English Composition, History of the Old Testament, History of New Testament. Tuesday and Thursday were lighter with courses in Christian Education, introduction to both Sociology and Psychology. The English grammar and essay writing classes helped to strengthen my skills for taking the O'level exam while the study in New Testament also provided clarity on some aspects of the religious studies I was about to write at the start of the New Year.

Time went by swiftly. When one is focused on a mission, it seems that there are not enough hours in a day to complete all that is required to be finished. September October, November all came and went rapidly. I had no health crisis even though the college campus was colder than my homeland.

End of term exams was the first half of December. Travel arrangements had to be made and tax exempt forms had to be procured in order to travel back home. I returned home and stayed with my sister for Christmas vacation and to write the exam in January of 1983.

I returned to Trinidad after taking the O'level in January 1983. Two new instructors came from Anderson, Indiana as missionaries to teach at the college – Dr. John V. Smith and his wife Margaret Smith. Also, four other female students were registered, two from Guyana and two from Trinidad.

Dr. Smith taught Church History, History of Israel, and Prophecy while Margaret taught Philosophy of Christian Education. Bro. Providence taught Psychology and Sociology and Bro. Drakes taught West Indian Literature and studies in Luke-Acts. His West Indian Literature class was the largest on campus since it was an experiment with a sister college – College of the Nazarene, whose students came on campus for the course. Bro. Payne taught *Koine Greek*, Hermeneutics and biblical interpretation, with concentration on preaching. Chapel service was scheduled from 11-12 each Wednesday.

In March of 1983, I received a letter from my sister Julienne informing me that I had passed all three subjects. For me, it was a great achievement due in part to the number of years I was out of school. Later, the certificate was posted to me for verification with the registrar. I switched from the certificate course to the diploma course in Pastoral Ministry.

Spring break came and classes suspended for the Easter break. The time was too short to go back home so I spent it on campus as did most of the New foreign students. The senior ones like Sis. Rhoda and Phipps from St. Kitts had families that they spent the time with. She spent hers with the James' in Tobago. On her graduation, she introduced me to the family and church, so that, if I needed, I could stay with them during the Christmas vacation.

Also in 1983, I learned through a telephone call from my sister Julienne about the passing of our Dad in New York. My emotions were ambivalent until the reality of his passing sank in, and I felt sad.

My fondest memory of him was the rides he would often give us on his bicycle whenever he came home to see us. Sometimes he would set us on the handle bar of his cycle and take us to his home. He had migrated before Mom to

England and would occasionally send us money. He seemingly left England and went to New York. At the point of the news of his passing, I had no idea how old he was since I did not know when he was born. As children, we could not ask such questions of our elders. I got to know my Mom's birth year when I had to work on applications requiring that information. However, for me, he was a kind and caring father within the limits and constraints of his resources. Were it not for that care and concern for me, I would not have had the surgery which, in effect, saved my life.

Having studied with the Smiths for the eighteen months they were there, they wanted to know what plans I had for the future and how they could continue to pray with me. At that time, all my focus was to finish the program and return home and work in the church, while I continued my civil service employment. They both felt that I had the ability to do well in my chosen path. Their friendship will prove vital at a later point in my development.

On completion of the school year, I travelled back to Antigua and stayed with my sister again for about six weeks. I went back to Customs and worked for that duration. I also went back to my home church on North Street and gave myself to ministry. For the weeks spent there, I taught bible studies, held prayer meetings, and minister the word during the evening services. I met with the pastoral leadership and was invited to attend the Ministerial Fellowship meetings.

Janice sent me a ticket from Tortola and we spent the next half of the summer together. It was a wonderful and sweet reunion; all three of us in union under the same roof, eating the same food and sharing thoughts that could not possibly be understood at a distance. Pernelle had grown a bit bigger over the two years but he had a speech difficulty. His word recall was limited. The pediatrician there said it was nothing to worry about, and that he would make adequate progress.

I started the new school year with a positive attitude. The routine was predictable and so I lost most of the stress and fear of not knowing. With instructor Sis. Cumberbatch, I took theory and practice of the fundamentals of Piano; Organization and Administration of Christian Ed., with Sis. Payne; Interpersonal Relationships, Evangelism, and the People We Teach with Bro. Providence.

During the Easter break, I took the ferry across to Tobago. My first ferry trip across the channel was stomach wrenching. I arrived there feeling nauseated and it took a few days for me to feel normal. I stayed with the James' and ministered in the local fellowship. They showed me around the interesting places of Tobago when they had time in the evenings after their work. Their home was warm and peaceful, and their care and appreciation of the stranger they viewed as ministry unto the Lord. Their home became a place where I would return several times over the years.

Studies continued. I did lawn care, kitchen duties, and learned how to bend steel for the making of decorative iron fences and gates under the tutelage of John Small. I also became the librarian. The library needed reorganization and I took that on as a project. In the first place, it was felt that the books we had were dated. Nothing much could be done in this regard except to ask sister colleges abroad for assistance. Second, it was also felt that periodicals and magazines would help students in their knowledge of what was happening in the wider world. Thus, letters were drafted and sent out to prominent members of congregations that supported the school. Calls were made to follow-up on mail contact. Individuals and churches saw the value and contributed to the project. Each commitment was for one year with a renewable clause for two additional years.

Magazine racks were built onto the wooden front ends of the book shelves for easy access of magazines. We received donations for one year subscriptions of Newsweek, Times, US News and World Report, along with the daily local newspapers.

Before the school year ended, I picked up a stomach virus. With it came a high fever which caused me to go to the doctor. On his examination, he felt that I needed urgent care and called for the ambulance to take me to the Port-of-Spain Hospital. Again, those who made assessment determined that my blood work showed a very low blood count and so transfusion was recommended. They administered antibiotics and two units of packed red blood cells along with hydration fluids over the five-day period I stayed in the hospital. This was the first time I was transfused and will not have another until 1994.

The school year ended and I returned to Antigua and did pretty much the same things; worked for half of the time with Customs and the church. I had my first vehicular accident driving home one evening from a meeting in Pastor Ivor Davis' new car. It was to be a short trip but turned out to be a lengthy evening. Traveling on American Highway, just past the Police Headquarters going south, I tried to overtake a truck going in the same direction when I drifted too close to it. The right side of the vehicle I was driving was badly damaged by the spiked wheel nuts of the truck that escaped without damage.

On my return to college in September of 1984, I was starting my final year. I would be required to do an internship with a local church for that year. When the assignments were posted, I was assigned to Huston Church of God where Pastor Frank Drakes was the pastor and the church located on campus. Duties included planning the chapel services for each week; visitation of the local membership that came on Sundays; planning and executing worship orders on Sundays as well as bible studies on Thursday evenings. There were a few baby dedications but there were no funerals or water baptisms; but I had to study the process just in case these were required.

In April of 1985, I received invitation to minister the sermon at the Women of the Church of God Annual Missionary Meeting, in Barbados. I accepted the invitation and began preparation for the event. I spent the weekend in the home of Pastor Lionel Gibson and his gracious wife.

Graduation was in May, 1985. My invited guests included Janice who came from Tortola, my Mom and sister Julienne who came from Antigua; and Joyce James who came from Tobago.

Before returning home after graduation, Janice and I took a week to travel to Tobago, this time by air in order to thank the church and the families that helped me during my years of study. We went to Tortola and spent three months before settling down again in Antigua.

On my return home, I reported back to work at the Customs Department of the Ministry of Finance. I had new responsibilities before long. I became a shift leader at the Baggage Room at the Airport.

Also, my home that was rented became vacant. I returned there to live and began plans for extension and renovation. The plan was to build a concrete blocks structure of one bedroom, one bath and a kitchen with the wooden section comprising the living room with the additional two bedrooms. The front would have an open porch. For this, I borrowed from Antigua & Barbuda Commercial Bank.

My contractor was my cousin Caleb Mullins who started the project in good faith but along the way got caught-up in more important work and did not finish the job. A friend of mine, Bro. Ash from Mount of Blessings Fellowship assisted me in completing the plastering of inside and outside the walled section. He also assisted me in getting the tiles down in the kitchen and bathroom areas; the septic tank and soak-away ready; and the installation of the bath and toilet fixtures.

My brother Vernon also assisted me in getting the electric wiring done. I installed a five thousand watts' step-down transformer to convert the entire home into 120 volts; this was necessary for all appliances that ran on that power.

In 1986, Janice's contract was fulfilled and she returned home with Pernelle. She also brought her car home as well.

Pernelle was registered in Sunny Side, a private school. We would soon find out that his behavior was out of synchronization with the rest of the class. He would do things to disrupt and draw attention to himself. We took him from that school and registered him in T. N. Kirnnon public school where he had the tendency to walk away and follow other children off campus. For his safety, we took him from there and had him registered in Zion Church School headed by Sis. Bernadette Roberts. This institution had fewer children and we believed that he would have fewer distractions in a smaller community. Yet, the problem persisted. He had a real difficulty sitting or standing quietly for the smallest number of minutes. He was fidgety all the time; without rhyme or reason he would not concentrate on any one thing for more than a minute, and he would become frustrated if asked to stay on task. His problem persisted all through his early schooling until a proper diagnosis came years later.

In 1987, changes were made in the Church of God Ministerial Fellowship. Pastor Ivor Davis and I were asked to take up congregational leadership positions at the Bethesda and St. John's congregation respectively.

The fellowship provided a new car – *Toyota Corolla* for ministry and a monthly stipend commensurate with the task. My commission was to visit with the membership on a regular basis in order to strengthen faith; preach the gospel of Christ each week with a desire for Christ to become the source of one's divine help; plan for prayer services and bible studies, baptize the converted and all the other things that are incidental to leading people in the way of righteousness.

In the summer of '87, The Caribbean Atlantic Assembly of the Church of God embarked on a program of sending Spot Missionaries to places that needed ministry assistance. Jamaica was identified as needing such help so I took three weeks off from work and went to Brown's Town, Abuka, and St. Ann's ministering and teaching as opportunity allowed. The next year, I was commissioned to Guyana to fulfill a similar assignment.

In June of 1989, I made my first visit to Anderson, Indiana, USA; to attend the International Camp Meeting of the Church of God. This was a gathering of leadership and lay people of the church around the world that came together for inspiration and renewal. I was fascinated and blown away by the professionalism and organization of the establishment; in worship, in teaching sessions, in appeal for missionary funding, in the commissioning of ministers to foreign missions. Many who came from Ohio and surrounding states lived on the camp grounds in recreational vehicles that were connected to electricity, water and sewage. Others stayed on the university campus in dorm rooms. I shared a room with the Caribbean Atlantic Assembly Director, Reverend Victor Babb from Barbados.

On the completion of an afternoon session that I attended, I was most pleasantly surprised to meet with Mrs. Margaret Smith. The very same lady who taught me Philosophy of Christian Education a few years earlier at West Indies Theological College, Trinidad. We talked about the intervening years. She related the death of her husband eighteen months earlier and how she was coping with his passing. I shared my ministry activities and experiences and the grace that was afforded me for each days' need of my journey. Then she raised the question of future study; to which I answered that I had no plans. She then suggested that I could explore the possibility of future study at the School of Theology; since exploration does not mean immediate commitment. She then gave me her contact information and said if I needed her assistance to give her a call. That evening, I prayed for guidance in the matter and the next day, I called her. Since it would do no harm in finding out the ramifications of future study, I asked her for her assistance. She informed me that she would make a few calls and get back to me. She did. She made an appointment for me to see the registrar Dr. James Bradley, and personally introduced me. Dr. Bradley outlined for me what the immigration policy that they were asked to follow in admitting foreign students. He outlined also the financial cost of study for the first year. He shared with me the course outline for the different programs they offered. He concluded by saying it would be a pleasure for me to study at the School of Theology based on his conversation with Mrs. Smith. I left the meeting with a bunch of brochures, application forms, and program schedules.

At the end Camp Meeting, Pastor Davis and I travelled by car with Pastor Malcolm and his Wife Chessie Phillip to spend three days with them in Clinton Springs, Cincinnati, Ohio. We had a wonderful time reconnecting. Though this was spring, the days for me were very cold and I was not particularly prepared for such change in weather conditions.

Thus, most of my trip was miserable in that I was discomforted by the cold.

The next leg on my expedition was by air to a church in Lake Wales, Florida. Again, I stayed in the home of Pastor Joseph De Hart who introduced me as speaker of their Sunday evening service. During my presentation, I made appeal for both financial and material resources for WITC in Trinidad. Out of this meeting came another informal meeting with a representative of Lake Wales Bible School who donated a number of newer volumes to WITC. All that was required was for me or WITC to arrange the freight cost to final destination. This was pursued via Pastor Davis who worked at that time with Leeward Islands Air Transport (LIAT). Half of the shipment was eventually shipped and reached final destination, but the rest did not, due in part to shipping cost.

I returned home all excited about the future. I share with the church my experiences of the two weeks away but nothing on the possibility of future study. I still had to fill the application, raise the six thousand US dollars needed to procure the student visa. With this in mind, I put in as many hours of overtime at the Customs Department that would help me realize this new challenge.

In September of '89, the car that Janice brought home from Tortola began giving a series of problems. We had to trade it in and did so under the auspices of the church; this was because as a pastor of a local fellowship, the government provided duty free status on such vehicles. We applied and got approval. We purchased a *Civic Honda* from Ryan Motors.

The year 1990 started with some anxiety. We wrestled with the issues of mortgage and car payments, Pernelle's learning and behavioral problems, and how my leaving would impact these issues. We were still trying to have a child after twelve years.

In March, I completed the School of Theology application, got the required referrals and pictures and sent on the completed package. Also, I shared with the congregation my desire to go back to school. Some members were dismayed; others ambivalent, while some others were quite disappointed. I was reminded in no uncertain terms that the church invested in my previous years of study and to get up and go was immoral. It was for me and the church like Kübler-Ross' model of five stages of dealing with death (denial, anger, bargaining, depression and acceptance).

Once my mind was at peace with the decision, I forged ahead with my plans. Family issues became more traumatic and congregational stability shaken. I received an acceptance letter in May with instruction on how to apply for my student visa. Fortunately, the US Embassy was located on Queen Elizabeth Highway which eliminated a trip to Barbados, where previously, all Lesser Antilles applicants had to apply.

On July 22nd, 1990, Pastor Ivor Davis and I were formally ordained as ministers of the church. It was an ecumenical affair with visiting dignitaries.

Also in July, I had the equivalent of the required funds in Eastern Caribbean currency with proof provided by bank statement. I went in and applied for the visa. On completion of the interview, I was awarded a three-year student visa to attend School of Theology, Anderson University in Indiana.

In my eagerness and naiveté, I made both pledge and promise to the church that I would return after my study and I had every intention so to do, not knowing what the future would be. Again, the government continued to grant me leave of absence for another three years without pay, holding my job until I returned.

I left Antigua on August 25th, 1990 to pursue a Masters of Divinity, a ninety academic hour adventure that would begin the following Monday. The school made arrangement for my pick-up from the airport; housing with another senior West Indian Student from Jamaica, Joseph Gordon. He took time to chaperone me around the city for the first week due to his ownership of a vehicle. He introduced me to the bus route, the places to shop, the bank that he was banking with, and some general information that proved helpful in time.

Registration and orientation was the first thing on the Monday. I registered for thirteen hours of classes since it was a requirement for a foreign student to take 12-15 hours or full load.

Students from different states, countries, and islands were gathered for this opening session. Professors gave out their syllabi and deliberated on their requirements. We were informed that all papers were to be typed and presented in the APA format. They spoke of their own hours when students could arrange for one-on-one meetings to discuss any problems. Students' were assigned academic advisors to assist with issues both academic and social. My advisor was Dr. Douglas Welch, a Canadian by birth, a former Missionary to Kenya, and professor of Anthropology and Multicultural Studies.

Mrs. Connie Albough was the financial bursar for students financing. Through her, I received scholarships and funding to cover my first year of tuition. In return, I wrote letters of appreciation to the donors and gave assurance that their investment in me would be shared with the wider church community in the Caribbean.

In preparation for the winter, I purchased thermal underwear. I applied for and got a campus job as a janitor during my first week of classes. As an international student, I could work on campus twenty hours per week in order to offset living cost. The rate was three dollars and seventy-five cents per hour and required me to be on the job at five o'clock in the morning. I worked until seven forty-five cleaning classrooms and restrooms in the Fine Arts building, and went to class for eight o'clock.

My schedule of classes for my first semester covered thirteen hours of class weekly, Monday and Wednesday; Tuesday and Thursday with an off day on Friday. It was expected that the off day would be used for researching and completing assignments.

Living cost was at first manageable. I paid one hundred sixty dollars per month for rent to Bro. Gordon for my attic room and half bath. I would shop for groceries and incidentals on a Friday. My cooking, washing, and cleaning skills came in handy so that my appearance was always to community standards.

It was expected that students carry medical insurance which I could not afford. My first experience with health issues was early winter of my first semester. Going out of the door one morning to work, I slipped off of the first tier of the slippery outside step and landed on my coccyx. Part of the reason for the slip was due to the tennis shoe I was wearing. The patteren grip of the sole had worn thin, having no grip. Since I had no insurance, I was reluctant to go to the doctor; but the pain was so excruciating that Bro. Gordon took me to see his physician. I had an x-ray and thankfully, nothing was broken. I was given strong pain killers for a few days. The pain remained long after the medication finished. In order not to have a repeat, I went and bought shoes that had the non-skid sole for winter.

I attended Park Place Church of God fellowship with Joseph Gordon who sang on the choir; because it was within walking distance. Attending services there was an eye opening experience in precision and professionalism. The greeters welcomed everyone as though they were old pals, remembering names even without name tags. The services started promptly on time, the elements were appropriately fitted together around the theme of the day, with outstanding coordination of traditional and contemporary music as well as the manipulation of lighting to change the mood and tone of each section.

I felt as if I was in an angelic atmosphere, filled with joy, far removed from my earthly cares, concerns, and frustrations for the ninety-minute duration of Sunday morning worship. I felt as though I was lifted up to another plain, similar to Paul's experience of being *caught up to the third heaven* (NRSV 2 Cor. 12:2).

My first understanding of the Thanksgiving celebration marked the historic importance and openhandedness of many in the community. I was invited to spend a portion of the day with another church family of German origin. The time was spent sharing stories of God's beneficence while at the same time our part in demonstrating God's care for the stranger. Table fellowship was one way in which barriers were broken down between class and race. The afternoon ended with games and prayers for each other's safety and prosperity.

I did not return home for Christmas. Instead, Janice and Pernelle joined me. It was exciting for all three of us in different ways. For me, it was a well-deserved reunion after not having the warmth of their face upon my face, the touch of their hands in mine; the fellowship of the table and all the little things we so often take for granted, but miss when they are taken away. For Janice and Pernelle it was their first experience of snow, and boy, did it snow! All three of us were exposed to the many concerts celebrating the birth of Christ. We viewed the fancy decorations of trees all over the university campus; we attended the beautiful orchestrated worship services, and the warmth of friends inviting us into their homes for table fellowship.

When I told David Kardasky, a fried I shared a couple of classes with, that my family was joining me for the Christmas holidays; he offered me his apartment for us to stay because he was going out of town for the break. This was an affirmation that God does work miracles in our lives, and just when we are most needy, He opens a door of opportunity. Again, I come back to the thought, that with God, all things are possible.

Christmas break was also a time of reflection on the end of my first semester, the grades I worked for and received, and the challenges that were to be faced in the new term. As the time drew near for Janice and Pernelle to return home, I thought about the best way to work on getting them to be with me at the beginning of the next school year.

Classes started early in January 1991. If I should finish the degree on time, I had to complete thirty hours in the first year. Since I only had thirteen hours the first semester, I needed to complete seventeen hours between spring and summer. I registered for fifteen hours with the hope of completing a practicum in Antigua on my summer break.

The heart of winter proved difficult for me in that I was bitterly cold all the time and even though I was warmly dressed, the wind chill was unbearable. I struggled with completing my assignments due to spending most of my indoor hours in bed, either with a terrible cough or some other allergy that kept me from functioning at my accustomed optimal pace. In March, just when I thought the weather was changing to spring, there came a terrible ice storm that knocked out the power at my home for about a week. Classes were cancelled for about three days since there was also no power on campus. Even though my writing and research were improved, I had poorer grades at the end of the semester due in part to the effects of the weather on my body and psyche.

Dr. James Bradley became my practicum supervisor for the summer course and arrangements were worked out to complete the three hour off-campus assignment with a satisfactory-not satisfactory grading. My remit was to set up a supervisory committee and meet with it once weekly. Also, a written progress report was due to him on a fortnightly basis. The objective was to evaluate the fellowship's present evangelistic program and make recommendations for improvements. The result would be a blueprint for adaptation and or implementation in other similar environments.

The semester closed around the middle of May. With my summer reading, assignment portfolio, and a few gifts and personal items; I purchased a return ticket and went home.

On arrival, there was a welcoming party outside the terminal building from the church consisting mainly of members of the youth fellowship. Their presence there and later that evening at my home indicated a slight change from the fear and apprehension shared a year earlier. This change of attitude was for me an affirmation that things were not as bad as previously indicated by the older members of the fellowship; which enabled me to both preach and teach in a challenging manner. As such, the persons I picked to be on the evangelistic assessment team were excited to serve, and that enabled frank and open discussion.

The Customs Department also welcomed me back to work during the summer months for which I was appreciative. It assisted me in making a financial contribution to my upkeep. It was quite a juggle to keep all of family responsibility, church activity, work schedule, and practicum studies going all at once; yet, God's grace continued to keep me going without having a physical or medical crisis. Looking back, I realize that determination to do well in order to succeed was a major factor. This was part of my work ethic from my growing up years. I believed strongly now as then, that nothing worthwhile having comes easy. It takes dedication and determination to succeed at every level of life. Once this is fully understood, all things are possible to those who are willing to invest their lives in the pursuit of their dream.

As the summer progressed, I discussed with my family the options of returning to school for the fall. After much prayer, we determined that it would be best for the family to be together for the additional two years of study. Once again, visas were procured for Janice and Pernelle to return with me.

We made arrangements for the rental of our home in order to keep paying our commitment to the bank. My sister again promised to help in this regard. She also consented to keeping the vehicle in good running condition while we were away.

We were again stepping out in faith into unchartered waters. The terrain was unfamiliar in that new arrangements had to be made for accommodation, school placement for Pernelle, the possibility of Janice getting to further her studies, and the financial cost associated with it.

In our back yard, we built a storage bin and packed away our belongings. I wound down my church activities, completed the assignment and began preparation for the next leg of study.

The night of August twenty-third, we were doing our final packing for our flight to Puerto Rico the following early morning; when there was a knock at the door. On opening, there was Mrs. Phillip of D. A. R. Phillip's Enterprise on Newgate Street. She ran her own clothing boutique on Coronation Road. Her visit was short; she came to wish me well in my studies. She handed me a card and left. We continued our packing until it was done. On her leaving, I opened the card, I found a cashiers' cheque in the sum of two thousand US dollars. It took my breath away for a moment. When I came to myself, I wiped my teary eyes and thanked God for the blessing.

We flew all day. We arrived in Puerto Rico and had to check in with immigration. From there we flew on to O'Hare, in Chicago, and from there to Indianapolis, arriving in Anderson late evening. We stayed the first few days in my one room attic dwelling until new arrangements could be worked out. Bro. Gordon was willing to let us stay in two rooms but the cost would be doubled. I found out through Connie Albough that there were family apartments at Mansfield and I should go directly to the supervisor and make my case. She was kind enough to call ahead of my coming and so it was that my application was approved the very day. The rental on the two-bedroom unit was two hundred twenty dollars monthly. We moved the next day. We bought second hand furniture from The Christian Center and began the second phase of building a family, making a home away from home. We also bought a second hand *Pontiac Wagon* for eighteen hundred dollars, which served us well.

I switched jobs from custodian and found employment in the Food Service Department. It was within walking distance from home. I worked nights from seven to twelve in the cafeteria at Holt Student Center four nights per week; serving drinks and sandwiches, cleaning tables, setting up and breaking down table arrangements for different functions.

We took Pernelle to register for school at Park Place Elementary. He was about ten years old but was placed in third grade until his records could prove otherwise. We explained to the teacher that he had difficulty staying in one place for too long and that he sometimes does things to seek attention. She promised to keep him fully engaged. At the same time, she said that there might be a possibility that he had some learning difficulties and might be better placed in special education. Time would prove her right.

About a month of Pernelle being in school, we were asked to come in for a consultation conference. From our communication and the school's in-house assessment, it was the considered opinion that Pernelle be seen by specialists who could diagnose, and hopefully treat his learning and behavioral issues. We agreed. Over the next several weeks, we were taking him from one psychologist to neurologist and behavioral specialists. The definitive diagnosis was Attention Deficit Hyperactivity Disorder (ADHD). The prescribed medication was in the main *Ritalin* in increased dosage until tolerance was established. Adequate rest, meaningful focused activity for short periods, and prescribed diet were also part of the regime. Since we were novices in dealing with this disability, counseling was an ongoing activity for the entire family for the rest of the period spent in Anderson.

Janice was eager to be either working in her profession or to be in school full-time. Neither was possible, at least, not until certain hurdles were overcome. To begin college, she needed to have a high school diploma or the equivalent of five GCE ordinary levels. Alternatively, she could do the General Education Diploma (GED), which she elected to do and successfully passed within two months. This opened for her the registration process at the university to peruse general studies.

Thus, from our arrival in Anderson in late August to the end of December 1991, we were all in school at different levels. We all faced difficult challenges in adapting to our new environment but we were also thankful for the blessings of being together as a family unit; the blessing of those persons that crossed our path; and particularly the blessing of those who put themselves out to assist us in the many and varied ways that made our lives bloom. With God, all things are possible.

"Lord Jesus, you have blessed the church with the gift of the Holy Spirit to empower and guide us through this vale of sorrow. His presence in my life has influenced and guided me to this point. Help me Lord to listen more keenly, trust Him more passionately, and obey His commands more enthusiastically, so that I may receive from Your hand the blessing of good health. You promised in Your word that if we knock, You will open the door; if we seek, we shall find You, and if we ask anything of You, we shall receive. Let Your peace be imparted to us in this new place as we wait for Your gracious hand of healing in our lives. Thank you Lord Christ, for Your continued mercies. Amen."

Chapter Five
I PRAYED FOR HEALING AND HE GAVE ME A GRAND OPPORTUNITY

".... My hope is in You," (Psalm 39: 7 NRSV). These words of the ancient psalmist are indicative of confidence that no matter the circumstances life brings, hope in God would be his strength. I have found that the hopeful person achieves much more than the pessimistic one. No matter how dark the horizon seems to be; no matter how stormy the seas of problems appear, the optimist never gives up hope.

Hope is defined as a strong desire to achieve or do something of importance; or to have something meaningful come out of a particular situation. It is the hope that through elected officials, the country, state, county, the city, be made more productive, having less unemployment, and greater health of the population at a reasonable cost. It is the hope or strong desire that each member of a family do what is ethically and morally right by fulfilling their potential through civic duty. It is the hope of the righteous that holiness will pervade each nation and that sin and unrighteousness is eradicated thorough virtuous living. Paul tells us that the Christian's hope lies firmly in the love of Christ. (Romans 5: 4-5 NRSV) "*...and endurance produces character, and character produces hope, and hope does not disappoint us, because God's love has been poured into our hearts through the Holy Spirit that has been given to us.*"

Many college students study with the hope of gaining skills and knowledge needed to make their mark on society, to make their corner of the world a little better in order to hand it on to the next generation. That was my hope, and to this idea, I received a lot of assistance from unexpected persons and places.

1992 for me started out full of hope. I made my fortieth year of life and thanked the Lord for journeying mercies. I was marking a milestone that I had no previous expectation of achieving, due in major part to by debilitating heath issues. And, here I was in the heart of an Indiana winter embarking on a new semester of graduate work.

I embarked on *Koine Greek* course, the language in which the New Testament was first written. This introductory course was taught by Professor Shievely. Not having a background in foreign language, it was, as the saying goes,

"This was Greek to me." I studied and struggled through each session doing my best to memorize the vocabulary, verb structure and endings, prepositional phrases, participles, and sentence structure. The harder I tried, the lower the grade on each weekly test I received. Yet, the professor was very encouraging and gave me tips to forge along. At the end of the course, I got my first *D* which meant that I had to retake the course in the summer.

I did not do any better with Biblical *Hebrew* either. To begin with, the page orientation in the Hebrew Bible is the opposite of our English Bible. In English we start reading the page left-to-right; the opposite is in Hebrew. From the alphabet to nouns and adjectives, I had a difficult time conceptualizing their construction. Dr. Timothy Dwyer was my professor who gave me encouragement and tips but the language to me was extremely confusing at the time. I also ended up with a *D* in the course and reregistered to take it in the summer.

I was asked to assist with the settling-in of two new West Indian students who arrived from Barbados and Jamaica respectively, to start of the 1992 school year. Bro. Chester Bridgeman attended West Indies Theological College in Trinidad where he was introduced to New Testament Greek and did very well. His desire was to complete the MA in

Biblical Studies which required two years of either Greek or Hebrew studies. Bro. Joseph Smythe came out of Jamaica to pursue the Master of Divinity with concentration in Christian Education. We became friends; I did for them what Bro. Joseph Gordon did for me when I first arrived on campus.

Our friendship enhanced each other, particularly my relationship with Bro. Chester who spent much time with me teaching me the rudiments of Greek and Hebrew so that when I took the retake of both in the summer, I was able to receive a passing grade to move on to the second half of each course.

Pernelle was doing much better on his medication and was improving in his school work. He was much more consistent in behavior and took responsibility for assigned chores. He taught himself to ride a bicycle; a lesson that I have never mastered at his age. He also learned to swim at the university's swimming pool. He developed and learned how to nurture friendship with other children on the compound while always looking out for the younger kid's safety.

Janice found work off campus. Through membership at Park Place Church, friendships were developed. In casual conversation with one of the members there, she was asked about her vocation. One thing led to another and recommendations were made to use her nursing skills in the home of a sick person the friend knew. She did such a marvelous job taking care of the patient at nights that when the patient finally died, another person was recommended to her.

Mrs. Gwinn's husband, Howard was a prominent pharmacist in the community with a chain of drug stores. He was paralyzed and needed twenty-four-hour assistance. Janice was recommended and became his night nurse. Since she could not be paid with a check or cash for her services, the Gwinn's worked out with the university a scholarship payment plan for her education. Thus, each pay period a check was deposited in her account at the university from which her tuition and our other expenses were paid. Through their friendship, Janice was trusted to drive their latest model Cadillac; take Mrs. Gwinn shopping and perform house chores as needed. She would take our Pontiac station wagon to get to work at seven and return at seven the following morning in time for classes.

I continued to be vigilant in managing my courses and family responsibilities as best I could. I worked as an itinerant preacher with appointments at churches such as Sherman Street Church of God; West Side Church of God; and a six months' leadership practicum in Hartford City First Church of God under the direction of Pastor E. Smith.

For graduation, two things were required in the final semester to graduate with the Master of Divinity with concentration in Pastoral Leadership. First, a student had to write an extensive paper on a theme that reflected one's theological perspective and its implications for ministry. I chose to write on the theme: *"Jesus' Ministry to the Poor as reflected in the Gospel of Luke 4: 18-30."* Second, a theological sermon had to be prepared, preached and critiqued by one's peers. I chose to preach on the *New Birth* from John's story of Nicodemus' nocturnal conversation with Jesus (John 3: 1-8). The preparation was excellent but the delivery was not as good, and the critique was helpful in reflecting that. Some said that it was too cerebral or intellectual and could have been more affective. Prior to graduation, there was a ceremony to recognize outstanding achievements. Quite a few students were recognized for their outstanding work in various fields such as working with children or in Christian Education. I was recognized for outstanding achievement in Bible Languages by the American Bible Society two years later.

Family, friends, and a few members of the church from Antigua came to my graduation in May, 1993. It was a proud and memorable occasion. The church members who came wanted to know how soon I would be able to return home.

They instructed that the church needed my input and that I should not hesitate to make known my future plans. It was an important water mark in my life's journey.

The first Sunday after graduation, on our way back from Hartford City, Indiana, we met with an accident. The car was badly damaged on the left side toward the back but we were not in the main injured or hurt, neither the other driver. Due to the car being a wagon, the impact was less severe on all of us. The other vehicle was also not badly damaged. We were indicating to turn in the left hand lane when out of nowhere we were struck from the rear left. The driver claimed that we turned into her vehicle. The insurance paid for her car repairs but we had to fix our own. For a while we tried driving it as it was, but it became inconvenient since the rear door and the left side door could not be opened, and the glasses on both sides were shattered. We finally traded it for a *Ford* that was barely drivable; it broke down before we reached home.

Since Janice had started a program at the under graduate level, and that Pernelle was doing better in school, I thought long and hard about the next step of our journey. Would it be wise now that I have completed my course of study to pull-up roots and go home? Would it be better to stay on for a while longer in order for Janice to finish her study and give

Pernelle a better chance to catch-up on his grades? Would it be better for me to go alone and leave them behind? How would they manage without my presence? These were my concerns and we prayed long and hard before deciding what to do.

The School of Theology through its human resources also wanted to know of my future plans. It appeared to me that the policy was for international students who benefitted from scholarships to return to their homeland as soon as they graduated. At the same time, the School of Theology was accepting applications into a two-year Master of Biblical Studies to start in the fall of 1993. I applied to pursue this program and was accepted. This was the best solution for the challenge in that Janice and Pernelle would have the opportunity to do their best in their respective studies for two additional years. This meant that I had to do an additional year of Greek and academic research.

I wrote to the church in Antigua. I explained my decision to delay my return as indefinite due to the reason of continued study. I also resigned my position as pastor so as to enable the church to move forward in finding new leadership. This development was not what they had anticipated and it caused a rift in our relationship. Nevertheless, it was for me the right thing to do at that time.

At the end of May '93, we moved from the Mansfield apartment complex to take up residence at 129 W 13th Street; a facility owned by 1st United Methodist Church who employed me as security and custodian. It was a minimum wage job but the housing and utility that came with it was a real benefit; a cost we never had to pay for the next two years. The two-story house was in a dilapidated condition but we worked to make it comfortable for us.

The job required me to be on site from 4:00-10:00 PM to open and close after daily activities; set up and break down seating arrangements for conferences, Sunday school, worship, small group meetings, funerals and weddings. On first Sunday of each month I had to prepare and set the table for communion and after worship wash the chalices and pack them away. During the school year, the church was like a bee hive with activities from morning till night. During the winter months the steps and walkways I had to clear of snow and ice.

In early November, I took a call from the chairman of a church pastoral committee to attend an interview in Powassan, Ontario, Canada. He was calling in response to my resume which I had forwarded earlier in the year. I explained that I was still taking classes and would not be available until the Thanksgiving break. He understood and we arranged to use that weekend for meeting. I showed Janice my routine at the church for that weekend and she graciously filled in during my absence. I travelled by Greyhound starting out at six-o-clock in the morning and arriving at my destination at eleven-thirty that night.

The fellowship at the Powassan church was around twenty all white elderly individuals, mostly women. Most had parents who started the fellowship and were interested in new leadership to evangelize their kids, grandchildren and great grandchildren. I got the impression that there was strong matriarchal influence which may have contributed to the lack of pastoral persons staying any length of time as leader, and probably, a new leader may well face some opposition in implementing new ideas too soon.

The following evening of my arrival was a revival meeting. It went well and I was congratulated many times for the relevance of the message that I shared. The day following, at around four-o-clock, we met at the church for the interview. They wanted to know my background and if I would consider leading a fellowship of that size and color. I indicated that size and color was never a problem for me since it was not for Jesus, who taught that we are to preach to all nations, creed, class, and ethnic backgrounds. They determined after the interview that they would like to meet my family and if I would consider coming and spending part of our Christmas vacation with them. They would provide board and lodging for us. I told the board it is something I would have to consult the family on and I needed time so to do.

I returned by bus four days later and we discussed the idea of going back to spend Christmas at the church. This was relayed to the chairperson and the time of travel was arranged, and a program of what would be done during our visit was worked out.

In my Thanksgiving weekend absence, the car we had broke down. Janice in her wisdom and initiative, found a reasonable *Toyota Camry* which she bought. Obviously, it goes without saying, that this vehicle had over a hundred thousand miles on it.

I went back to my routine of classes and my work schedule at the church until the Christmas vacation. I had arranged for and walked Joseph Smythe through the routine of my job so he could fill in for me during our absence.

On December 22nd we packed bags of clothing and things we thought we would need to spend a week in Canada.

We serviced the vehicle before leaving. Then we ventured forward in confidence that it would take us and bring us back safely.

Travel was easy following the route by map. The first leg of our journey came to an end in Troy, Michigan, around three-O-clock where we stayed by a retired Pastor friend of the church to which we were headed. We were warmly greeted, welcomed into their home and fed sumptuously. After dinner, we were engaged in conversations about the church and what to expect if we were to be called to serve. In the morning, we were refreshed with breakfast and packed lunches for our second leg of the journey. We started out at seven.

We passed through immigration check point and got clearance to proceed. After travelling about an hour on the M 4 N into Canada, we heard rumblings under the hood of the car and saw steam belching. We pulled over onto the shoulder and stopped. Lifting the hood, we observed that the radiator cap blew off and the steamy water pouring out. fortunately, we had bottled water and refilled the radiator and corked it with a rag covered in foil. This slowed us down a bit but with no further mishap; we arrived safely at our destination around ten thirty the same evening. On our arrival, it started snowing lightly.

The chairman of the board met us at the manse which they had prepared for our stay. We were exceedingly cold and tired so he asked us to drive into the garage and provided us with an engine-block plug for us to plug the car into the receptacle to prevent the engine from freezing. On his departure, we gave thanks for the blessing of the day, for friends who assisted us, and for what we were about to experience in the days ahead. We tucked ourselves into the upstairs beds and had no difficulty in falling asleep.

We awoke late Christmas-eve and to our surprise, the snow fall had accumulated three-to-four feet high blocking the window. We had never seen or felt snow like this before since it was like grains of uncooked rice, and just as dry. Again, the chairman was out early clearing the driveway and walkway for us. During the course of the day, we were able to see a little of the town. We drove around on our own. We found an auto shop and got a new radiator cap. We also bought oil and gas from a petrol station. We bought from some Native Indians, handmade scarves, hats and gloves.

In the evening was the Christmas pageant put on by the children of the church. The attendance was around fifty persons, some of whom were relatives and parents of the children. My participation came at the close; whereby I introduced my family and said the closing prayer. I saw that there was potential for growth if all the people in attendance that evening were to be contacted and followed- up on a regular basis. It would of course be a challenging task, but one that most certainly would bear fruitful reward.

On Christmas day, the service was at 9:00AM. Many of those who came for the Christmas pageant the previous evening came. I spoke on the significance of Christ's coming into our world from the Gospel of John 1: 1-4 KJV. The response was graciously measured in keeping with the purpose for which we were there. We were invited to a luncheon interview with the women's group, who put on a spread in keeping with the Canadian Christian hospitality.

Again, it was an occasion for us to share with the group and leadership our national background; our spiritual journey; our future plans for ministry. They wanted to know what considerations we would give to be of service to the congregation if it was the Lord's will that we become the pastors; and how we would cope with winters that were longer than the ones we had already experienced in Anderson. We discussed schooling for Pernelle and possible work for Janice in her nursing field. After about ninety minutes of discussion, the chairman closed the meeting by praying for the leading of the Holy Spirit and the wisdom needed to guide the fellowship forward.

One of the younger members of the women's group offered to take us around the day following for us to get a feel of the community. We were shown a few schools and drove into North Bay and Halifax, about twenty-five minutes away to see one of the hospitals. The last service was held on New Year's Eve, my final assignment. At the end, the chair indicated that they would be in touch with us as they would meet and make their final decision.

On New Year's Day, we said our final goodbyes, packed up and headed back home around 6:00 AM. We made good time getting back on the M 4 S as we chatted about the experience and challenges ahead. The farthest thing from our minds was another break down. But it happened.

At about 3:00 PM the car began losing power, slowing to a crawl on the highway. I managed to slowly maneuver the vehicle from the middle lane to the shoulder and before I could stop, it stopped on its own accord. There was no smoking when we lifted the hood. There was sufficient gas to take us onto S 95 into Indiana. Not having membership coverage, and cellphones not yet available, we just stood by the vehicle and tried stopping anyone that would probably give us assistance. For about an hour no one stopped. We were freezing in the cold, so we determined that Pernelle and Janice would stay in the car for warmth while I tried to get assistance. We would then rotate standing outside while the other warmed up. All the time I was praying for someone to stop and assist us.

As our anxiety increased, we were becoming frantic due to the darkening of the oncoming evening. Another fifteen minutes passed before a car stopped. The man pulled up ahead of our broken down vehicle and came to us. He introduced himself as Mr. Al Yeo and enquired what was the problem. We explained to him what we thought was the problem. He thought that the oil was low and that the gas meter may be defective not giving the proper reading; thus, he took me in his vehicle to the nearest gas station and we bought gas and oil. We returned and poured them in. After several attempts, the car still would not start. He suggested that we needed to get the vehicle to a repair shop but it being a holiday, none would be opened. He was a blessing to us in many ways. From a pay phone he called for a wrecker to tow the car to the garage that he serviced his car and took us in his vehicle to his home to spend the night, since we did not have the financial resources to check into a hotel.

Next day, the mechanic called to say that the head gasket was blown and the part needed to fix the problem was not available. It was his hope to have it in a day or two. He indicated that the cost of repair was three hundred and forty dollars CND. Again, we did not have that much money to pay it all at once so we gave Mr. Yeo the one hundred and fifty CND we got from the church and promised to forward the balance once we were able in a week or two. He accepted. We fulfilled our promise and we stayed in touch with that family until we lost touch with them in 2002.

The entire experience helped us to affirm our trust in God and the goodness of humanity as the psalmist declared. For many times God uses others to show his might and power to deliver out of the hand of devastating circumstances. While standing on the road in the cold, I imagined quite a number of other dark scenarios. For example, no one stopped and we would all freeze to death in the cold car since our body heat had already depleted. Or, someone stopped and abduct us for malevolent purposes. But that was not God's plan for us at that time. He selected the right person who had the right connections and resources to give assistance. Apart from affirming my hope in God, I also made it a point in my life from that day onward, to increase my benevolence and hospitality to strangers. Many things can cause us to be stranded on the road of life and we are to be like the Good Samaritan; risk our lives and resources to aid those who have fallen by the wayside.

The early parts of '94 brought a heavy snow storm and ice rain but we were kept warm, employed, and motivated to finish our pursuits. Pernelle was performing much better in his school and Janice was enjoying her study at the undergraduate level. The chairman called in February and explained that they made a decision not to call us to ministry and wished us success in our endeavors. On receiving the information, I sent another resume/application to a church in London, England, that advertized for leadership.

During the summer of '94, I registered and completed the second year of Greek classes in preparation for the MA in Biblical Studies. It was difficult working and studying at the same time but persistence paid off in the long run.

On a summer Saturday morning while working at the church preparing for a wedding to be held in the evening, I began having stomach pains and diarrhea. I took some medication and over the counter pain pills to alleviate the discomfort, but it persisted and became progressively worse as the day wore-on. I also had a fever. At around 10:00 PM, when I closed the church after everything was accomplished, I went directly to bed with the discomfort.

Sometime in the night, my wife told me that I was talking in my sleep saying something like, *"I can't make it, I can't make it!"* She noticed that my breathing was labored and I had an elevated temperature. Around 4:00 AM, she decided to take corrective measures; she woke Pernelle, and both maneuvered me to the car. Later when I became conscious, she told me that herself and Pernelle practically dragged me to the car, got me in, dragged me out at the hospital and took me to the emergency room. She said by the time I was placed on a stretcher, I was unconscious and did not respond.

At the hospital they ran tests and found out two things. First, they found that I was having a bout of pneumonia, for my lungs were filled with fluid. Second, and most critical, for all intents and purposes, when they checked my hemoglobin it was as low as that of a dead person; the reading was (2.1). For those who have a general knowledge of the composition of blood hemoglobin, it is common knowledge that any normal male individual would have a blood hemoglobin count between 13-17 points. Also, normal blood cells have a lifespan of about four months. In my case, it was found that their lifespan was now about thirty days. The doctor who admitted me was surprised that I was still alive and breathing with the count that low. Added to that, they discovered that my blood cells were not of the Cycle Cell formation as given in the assessment by Janice. On running a second blood test, they confirmed that the formation of my red blood cells fitted the pattern and formation of Beta Thalassemia Major[2], a genetic disease affecting less than two hundred thousand people around the world; and found more in the Mediterranean area than in the Caribbean. For example, in Cycle Cell Anemia, the Cycle Cells are incomplete circles, more elongated in shape and have the tendency to stick together rather than sliding over each other, causing congestion and pain in the joints. On the other hand, Beta Thalassemia cells are immaturely developed, having hollow nucleuses and thus carrying less oxygen. Beta Thalassemia in its range of stages can be mild to severe, and have two or more mutations of the DNA cells that make hemoglobin. It is also a progressive disease in that the longer it goes on, the more severe it becomes. The physicians' at that time questioned me about my family's medical history and background; they wanted to know if any of my parents were ever sick and needed to take

---

[2] See comprehensive presentation of *Guidelines for The Clinical Care of Patients with Thalassemia in Canada*. Published by the Thalassemia Foundation of Canada. www.thalassaemia/ca/wp-contentupload

transfusion. I relayed that My Mom was never sick and I did not know of my Dad being in the hospital at any time needing transfusion. None of my other siblings ever had it either. The physicians view was that I will need to be transfused regularly since there is no other way to deal with the regular mass destruction and break down of the red blood cells.

Antibiotic medication was applied to relieve the congestion in my lungs, oxygen and two units of red packed blood cells were given to keep me alive. The next day, new x-rays and other imaging of my chest and abdomen were taken; I was treated with another two units of blood with oxygen. I spent six days in the hospital and racked up a bill of ten thousand dollars; because we had no medical insurance. We were instructed to apply for indigent assistance through charitable organizations to help with paying the bill. Gradually some funds came in and we were able to pay half of the cost.

Sometime in August, while I was at home recuperating, I took a call from the London church from Reverend Everard Harvey. Again, he wanted an interview and so we settled for this to take place during the Christmas vacation. He outlined an itinerary for worship and retreat to last four days away from the church.

What I failed to do was to check the status of my visa before leaving, and this will be to my detriment when I was ready to return.

I boarded British Airway in O'Hare, Chicago, for my first transatlantic flight. I arrived at Heathrow airport the following morning and was met by Brother Espert Green and sis. Thelma Khan. Traveling across times zones does take its toll on the body, because I slept quite a lot in the van on our way to Tottenham. On reaching St. Ann's Road, I met a group of women who had been awaiting my arrival with prepared lunch. We chatted for a while exchanging pleasantries and family talk. The place where I was to stay was in the country with the Harvey's and he was picking me up after his work around five PM. They were very gracious hosts, and would continue to be so toward us during our ministry years there.

Again, I was briefed on the schedule: I was to minister the word on Sunday; on Christmas Day, and minister and teach the word at the retreat to be held at a hotel in Herne Bay, near Canterbury, southwest England.

I really had a marvelous time of preaching and teaching in the fellowship and at the retreat. I had learned a few tips from a little pamphlet on *succeeding at interviews* which came in handy.

At the interview, the committee outlined their concerns. The top four concerns were evangelism and outreach to the community, with focus on growing the membership; youth programs that would grow the faith of children and youth already in the fellowship, and those who would become members at a later date; visitation of the general membership, particularly with the senior members who may be hospitalized or are unable to attend worship on a regular basis. There was also concern for integration and inclusion of members from other national backgrounds.

I responded to the first concern with reference to John 1: 35-51 NIV where John pointed two of his disciples to Jesus. Andrew went and called his brother Simon and introduced him to Jesus. This is what I called *Family Friendship Evangelism* at that time. The principle is straightforward in that it places the obligation on everyone in the fellowship to play a vital role in church membership development.

Many congregations think and subscribe to the unspoken principle that it's the pastor's major role to be that of evangelist in bringing new people into the fellowship;

but that is not entirely the case. His or her role is to train the members to do their part in helping them to bring their own family members and friends to Jesus. My own experience has borne this out in that Janice invited me to *"Come and See."* I went and saw and committed my life to Christ and never looked back since. I, as an individual member of a fellowship invited others of my family and friends and they came, saw, and given their lives to Christ. I sensed that this idea was not well received and engendered lengthy discussion and diverted attention into other areas. But at least it got the leadership to begin thinking of new ways in which evangelism could be done.

I addressed the second concern of youth development by asking what was in place and what resources would be made available for such a program. I learned that there were interested persons who would volunteer their time to be trained in Christian Education with emphasis on children and youth. I suggested that this would be ideal if funds could be made available for putting a program together. The church hosted a group of Tri-S Anderson University students each summer for a five-day Vacation Bible School; but there was little or no follow-up on completion. I suggested that the follow-up aspect was vital for keeping interest of the youth. It would be my proposal to train those who worked in the Sunday school to become a part of a team to develop a youth program.

The third concern would take some time for me to get to know where the elderly resided and or the hospitals and care homes where they were placed. I suggested that help would be needed by someone who had knowledge of the city and the places where membership resides until I was sufficiently oriented to do visitation on my own.

The fourth concern of integration and inclusion of members from other national backgrounds would include having representatives take ministry responsibilities on boards, committees and task forces. Also, volunteerism is a great way to encourage all to participate and take ownership of the fellowship. I also suggested that we need to tread carefully by not legislating or try to force people who may not want to take leadership role in the fellowship. Such responsibility must be led by the Holy Spirit and freely accepted by the individual for effective performance of tasks.

On completion of the interview, I stayed with Sis. Thelma Khan for travel back the next day to Anderson. On reaching the check-in, I was informed that my visa to the USA was expired and needed renewal. The airline attendant graciously gave me an extension on the ticket if I could get the visa issue sorted out. Thus, I was taken back to the city of London to the embassy for the renewal. Fortunately, Sis. Khan knew where to go and we were able to procure the new visa same day. I called Janice to let her know not to go to the airport since I did not make the flight. I told her of the mishap and assured her that the next day I would arrive at the same time. The following morning, we went back to Heathrow and I was able to board the flight back to Anderson.

I registered for classes which started 6th January 1995. Worked and studied for the completion of the course work needed. Janice did the same and Pernelle was making plenty progress in his classes. No news came from the London church even though I had hopes of hearing a positive word. January, February and March ended with no word. I celebrated my forty-third year of life with no prospect of finding gainful employment. But I kept on hoping. Spring was late in coming for up to mid-April we still had bitterly cold weather with intermittent snow days.

One afternoon early May, it could have been fifth or sixth of the month, about two-o'clock, I was reading for one assignment when the telephone rang. I answered and it was Deacon Harvey of the Tottenham Church in London on the other end. We exchanged pleasantries before he broke the news that the board had made its decision. He informed me that the decision was to call me to serve as their pastor. A letter of call was on its way with instructions in procuring entry certification. I responded with delight and said I would call him back within a few days as there was completion of study issues for us.

That evening we shared the information and began sorting out how we would complete our studies. Janice was in process of finishing her AA and would graduate in June. I was completing the last nine hours of general course work with a thesis pending. Pernelle was in ninth grade at middle school and I feared that taking him out of school when he was just getting settled would not be the best choice. We however, gave thanks for the prospect of serving in London, England.

I discussed with my academic advisor Dr. Timothy Dwyer and my academic coach Dr. Douglas Welch the possibility of serving in London and that I would need time to complete thesis. Since the proposal was accepted, I was granted two years to complete it with reporting progress quarterly.

A week later the invitation letter arrived and I responded with acceptance of the offer. Letters and calls went back-and-forth for some time. Eventually, we checked out the air fares which we had to purchase on a reimbursed method. We sent and received back our passports from British Consulate, Chicago with entry certificates for one year. Janice graduated in early June with AA in General Studies and we informed our new employer that we would arrive there June 29th 1995.

Praying for good health and healing for over forty years became natural for me on a daily basis. Jesus had said, *"When you pray believe!"* I prayed for healing and God in His wisdom gave me a grand opportunity in London to serve His people.

We resided at the church's manse located at 6 Branksome Avenue, Edmonton, London for six-and -a-half years. Members took time to orient us to the city, bus and underground connections, shopping, and schools in the area for Pernelle.

I got in touch with my half-brother and half-sister St. Clare and Margolyn respectively. Margolyn and her family lived in Chrystal Palace, South London. St. Clair and his family lived in Leicester. Also, I got in touch with my half- brothers on my father's side; Phillex and his family; and his brother Quenelle and his family; they also lived in Leicester. Janice got in touch with her Aunt Chris and extended family who also lived in Tottenham. These connections helped us to settle-in and they provided stability for our first couple of years.

As humans, we were excited to be in London but gradually we started comparing and noting the differences from where we came. We appreciated the fact that we had the opportunity to be covered by a health care system that offered services without direct charge or insurance. We received our National Insurance cards within six weeks of our arrival. We were registered at a GP's office within walking distance of our home as well as having the North Middlesex Hospital not very far away from home as well. On my initial visit to the GP, he recommended that I see the hematologist Dr. Yardumine at the North Middlesex Hospital where the unit for treatment was located.

Another difference we noted was the efficiency of the transport system. We found the cost of travel on both the bus and underground very reasonable and we could get around with ease because of the scheduling. Also, we noted the laid-back manner of the people. They seem to us not to be in any great hurry in doing things. This I gradually came to appreciate and practice.

Our contractual arrangement with the church administration for home expenses was unique. The home was furnished. We paid for our own cable and the church paid half of the telephone cost. We fully paid for water and electricity on a quarterly basis. The church paid a reasonable salary commiserated with the responsibilities and provided a vehicle; they paid for the car's maintenance, and the cost of petrol was split 50/50. Initial contract was for one year and possible renewal annually.

We were installed as pastors in September of 1995. It was a grand celebration with invited guests from surrounding churches making it somewhat of an ecumenical affair. I spoke on the call of Isaiah, from Isaiah 6: 1-9.

The church launched its Building Fund Project in March 1996 to extend the church's ground floor from the back and put on a balcony on the extended portion. The project was cost out at one hundred and fifty thousand pounds.

Janice had to go through a conversion adaptation course to practice nursing in London, which she successfully completed within the prescribed time. She applied and was employed at the North Middlesex Hospital, mid-April, 1996.

Pernelle had to go through new school assessments and did not get into a regular class until February of 1996. We were allowed to drive on our Indiana licenses for thirty days after which we needed UK licenses. I got mine in February of 1996 and Janice got hers three months later.

In September of 1996, I was hospitalized with shingles on an isolation ward at the North Middlesex Hospital. I spent nine days on the unit and was advised on discharge to take an additional two weeks to recuperate. One of the physicians told me that my condition attracts opportunistic diseases; in other words, due to a compromised immune system, I will catch whatever is in the air, and such things will perplex my life on a continuous basis.

In the summer of 1997, I returned to Anderson for presentation and critique of thesis: *Ιλατηρίον: in Israelite Religion and a Mythological Interpretation of the Concept in Paul's use in Romans 3: 21-31*. After lengthy discussion, certain section needed only a rewrite while the first two chapters needed new research. Project was completed and degree awarded in absentia 1998. Also in this year, I repaid the balance of my hospital debt to St. Johns Hospital, Anderson, Indiana.

In the summer of 1998, I took ten days leave to go to Antigua with Pernelle. Prior to this vacation, he was asking questions about his being adopted and what it meant. So we explained it to him and so he wanted to get to know his birth parents. This trip was for him an eye- opener. Over the years, we had kept in touch with his mother and the day I introduced him to her, she was overjoyed in meeting him. He was approaching his eighteenth birthday. He spent most of the time in her home and met his other siblings and father.

I enjoyed ministry immensely for about the first four years or so. I got to know my congregation and they became more knowledgeable of us as we interacted on a weekly basis. We still have many friends there who took the time to personally care and minister to our physical and spiritual needs.

The fellowship was on average two hundred members of different professions such as school principals, nurses and hospital administrators, transport and civil servants, retirees, college students and children. But this was also a multinational fellowship with members of various Caribbean nation peoples such as Jamaicans, Trinidadians, Barbadians, and Vincentians.

And, from continental Africa, were Kenyans, Nigerians, Zimbabweans, and their children who were born and raised in England.

Administratively, the church was managed by a Board of Trustees that dealt with the business side of the church to which I was invited periodically in an advisory capacity. The Pastoral Committee assisted the pastor in dealing with issues and plans to move the fellowship forward. Thus, representatives for this entity were selected from the leadership of the Women of the Church; the Men's Fellowship; the Sunday School Superintendent; Youth and Children's Ministry. This body would meet on a monthly basis chaired by myself and reports tabled as to what was accomplished from previous agenda.

Part of my giving back to the community was volunteering as a Chaplain for one hour twice per week for about eighteen months. This assignment was supervised by Rev. Rose who was main chaplain for North Middlesex Hospital. I did this on ward six ministering to the patients with HIV/AIDS. They were mostly Europeans and Africans who had the resources to travel to London for treatment.

In our monthly meetings, I thought of myself as a listener and gave my advice on the particular matter at hand accordingly, be it on a personal or congregational basis. In one Pastoral Board meeting around 1999, I was told by a member of the board that I was not a synthesizer in my thinking. In her mind, I saw things only in a lineal manner, and I suppose she was right, in that I saw action bringing about reaction. My tendency was to study the consequences of an action before taking that action, always looking for a better alternative with a more satisfactory outcome. In those days, I wasn't a person pleaser; I endeavored to do what I considered right for the best outcome.

Thus, there were times when we did not see eye-to-eye on an administrative level. Yet, there were no animosity or friction in the leadership due to this critique. I took it under advisement.

In 1999 also, the World Conference of the Church of God was held in Birmingham, England. This was a gathering of church leaders held every four years to firstly, look back and report on accomplishments; secondly, to look forward and plan ahead globally. It was also a time to select new leaders for the different areas or zones in which the church had an interest.

We had to renew our certificate of residency each year at the Home Office. When we applied for our extension of stay in 1999, the officer at the Home Office determined that we were eligible for permanent residency status. We filled out the forms and sent them in. When we receive them back we became British Nationals in the year 2000. We applied for United Kingdom passports and receive same a couple of weeks later.

At the same time, there were congregational issues that caused strong feelings to boil over among the membership. Some disliked the worship style and others the preaching style, still some others disliked not being given time and opportunity in each service to express their views through testimony. Thus, many departed to other fellowships. In my view, these issues were not unique to our church, since they are perennial problems of church life over the years; and will continue to be so till the end of time.

One of the high water marks of the fellowship, and to some extent my ministry, was its missional focus. We raised monies for the support of West Indies Theological College (WITC) in Trinidad for two years and for Phyllis Newby's Ministry in Haiti for another two years. It happened that WITC needed a spot missionary to assist with instruction. Deacon

Harvey who became a retiree was interested and so we worked on the details and he spent two years with the institution.

Another high-water mark of ministry was that I acted as instructor of Practical Ministry during the summer for students who were finishing their degree at Church of God Colleges. The first student was Andre Machael from Germany. He spent the designated six weeks with the four- congregations learning the practice of ministry in a multicultural setting. This required living in the home of the hosting pastor, doing the work of visitation both in home and hospital; crafting and leading worship, preaching the word and bible study, baptisms and baby dedication along with funerals and weddings, as opportunity allowed.

The student also had to keep a journal of task completed and the pastors provided a written evaluation so that I could compile a satisfactory or unsatisfactory grade to the student's institution.

In the second year of the summer program, Clive Williams benefitted from it out of WITC. The third person was Cloyde from the same institution.

Gem Brown was a member of the East London fellowship who wanted to finish her studies in Theology and so we recommended her to WITC. She applied and was accepted, spent two years and graduated.

I also supervised short courses for ministers who were not ordained. Bro. Basil Callender of the East London Church went through the classes whereby we met one-on-one for a three-month period. On successful completion, he was ordained to ministry.

At the dawn of 2001, I had the strong feeling that time was limited for continued ministry. The main issue was church growth or lack thereof. The congregation was mostly peopled with persons of West Indian extraction in majority, and others of African countries such as Nigerians, Kenyans, and Zimbabweans were minority. The West Indians were more vested in leadership positions and this may have given rise to alienation of others. Also, worship style of those of African descent required lots more music and dance time with prophetic declarations which; gradually was limited. Added to this, the majority of the congregation had to travel great distances to get to worship, many by train and bus. My error was probably holding our main worship to ninety minutes on Sundays rather than the long-lasting one they were accustomed; with and evening sixty minutes one. The greater attendance came for the eleven o'clock service and sometimes came late with the hope of a drawn out service to meet their need. Sermons were often not protracted – about half the worship time, and by twelve thirty, the service was ended. We spent many hours in administration discussing these issues.

I was unable to successfully integrate into leadership those of African ancestry which may have contributed to their leaving the fellowship.

Nevertheless, under my ministry, Aunt Chris and her family began coming regularly. One afternoon after visiting a member on Fore Street, Edmonton, I met a young Christian lady that I should have known by name but did not recall at the time. She remembered me by name and reminded me that I had ministered to her church in Port-of- Spain, Trinidad in the 80s, when I was a student. She reminded me also of ministering to her at a youth camp held in St. Kitts a few years later. Well, I shared with her that I was the pastor of the Tottenham church located on Plevana Crescent off St. Ann's road, and invited her to come. Her name was Maria Phillips. She came with her husband and child. From that first visit, they stayed and are still an integral part of the fellowship.

During or just after the volcanic eruption on the island of Montserrat, West Indies, in 1997, the Simpson family were relocated to London. They resided in a home provided for them adjacent to the church. Mrs. Simpson, a Christian lady, came with her five children one Sunday morning, liked what she saw and heard, and stayed. The fascinating thing about this story is that she and the entire family came morning and evening as well as the mid-week service.

Also, in the complex where she lived was a former member who had stopped church attendance, so I visited and encouraged, and he renewed his commitment to Christ, and he is still in attendance at the time of writing. Charles McCoy was a prominent elderly member of the fellowship when I was first installed. He was seemingly appointed to assist us with any maintenance needed at the home. He introduced me to Jean, his intimate friend. She never attended on a regular basis but with time and counseling, she became a regular member; accepted water baptism; and I was fortunate to marry them a year later.

I took three weeks' vacation in May 2001 and went to Decatur, Georgia, to visit my friend Norris Ferris. I had applied for an advertised position with United Church of God in Toledo, Ohio. Thus, we would travel by car up to the church and spend the second weekend of my visit with the church. The interview went well and on my return to London, I was offered the position to minster there. The issue that caused the call to be rescinded was the churches' inability to provide visas for the entire family.

In June of 2000, we bought our first car – *Nissan Micra* with two doors. This was our first purchase of a decent vehicle in London. It had seven miles on it. It was also very economical with petrol.

At the same time, we were pursuing the possibility of in-vetro-fertilization or IVF. The doctor was of the view that age will be a great concern for the baby's viability, thus we decided not to go further with the idea.

In August of 2001, Janice and I went to Leicester where new homes were being constructed. Phillex took us around to see the building sites and we settled on the Thorp Astley site where duplexes were being built. We purchased unit thirty with a twenty percent down payment of cost; and saw construction from foundation up. Completion time was three months.

Janice attended a recruitment fair held in West London in the year 2000. She placed her resume with South Florida Health Systems and was called for an interview three months later. From that initial interview, paper work was initiated to find placement for her with the company; which eventually came through in October 2002.

Pernelle had completed his special education classes and finished school in 1998. He chose a vocation path in sales and service and was assigned with different companies as volunteer for experience purposes. At the same time, his social worker advised that he be given greater freedom in making his decisions in order to develop independence. It was their view that he be given the opportunity to be on his own. This process took some time to find the right location to meet his needs. We give thanks to God, blessed be He, for the help of Mrs. Iota Phillips-Callender who worked tirelessly on Pernelle's behalf to get him the right residential location.

By September 2001, the Board of Trustees meeting was held and I was informed that my contract was not going to be renewed. Thus, I wrote my resignation letter to the Board effective immediately. Seemingly, the Board did not expect a resignation so quickly, thus, we negotiated and came to a compromised leaving date three months after.

At the farewell service, I was showered with praises for the work I did and I thanked those who worked along with me to make whatever improvements were accomplished. I also instructed that continued efforts be made to raise the additional sums for the building renovations as well as the employment of ministry gifts in the fellowship to build-up each other's faith.

We packed up our belongings on the 30th day of November 2001 and moved into our new home in Leicester. Before leaving, we settled Pernelle in his new living quarters which housed other youths with disability.

In retrospect, I prayed for healing, and faith enabled ministry in an international city with a challenging life in London. God gave strength and wisdom to take the opportunities that came my way.

> *"The blessing of the Lord makes rich and adds no sorrow," says Solomon (Proverbs 10: 22 NIV).*
>
> *Over the years, I have prayed for health and healing, and You have blessed me with family and friends who have enriched my life to this day. You have led me to understanding and knowledgeable physicians who provided compassionate counsel, and treatment, enabling me to have a better quality of life. I pray for*

them and their work that, You may continue to use them in effective ways of bringing life and health to others. Help me not to forsake their instruction, their kindness, their love, their support that has contributed so much to making my existence enjoyable, pleasant and rewarding.

Truly, as Paul says, (and I paraphrase), "It is in you that I live, and move, and have my being, (Acts 17: 28 NIV). I humbly ask that, You continue to be gracious to my family and friends. Grant them the joy of knowing that You will reward them in this life, and in the life to come, eternity. Thank You for all you have done for me in Jesus' name. Amen.

Chapter Six

I PRAYED FOR HEALING AND GOD GAVE ME A NEW FELLOWSHIP

There are many biblical examples of prayer answered directly, providing what was requested. A case in point from the Old Testament is Hannah's prayer for a man child. *"O LORD of hosts, if only you will look on the misery of your servant, and remember me, and not forget your servant, but will give to your servant a male child, then I will set him before you as a nazirite until the day of his death,"* (1 Samuel 1:11NRSV). She in due season, received her request and sang praises to God, who looked upon her oppression. Another example is that of Solomon who prayed for understanding and wisdom in leading God's people (1 Kings 3: 5-14) and was answered. A third is found in 1 Chronicles 4: 10 (NIV), '*Jabez cried out to the God of Israel'*: "*Oh that you would bless me and enlarge my territory! Let your hand be with me, and keep me from harm so that I will be free from pain."* And God granted his request.' Yet, there are other examples in scripture where prayers are not directly answered as immediately, or in the manner of need. For example: in the New Testament, Paul's prayer for his thorn in the flesh to be removed, but it was not taken away at all. (2 Corinthians 12: 7-10 NIV). *"Therefore, in order to keep me from becoming conceited, I was given a thorn in my flesh, a messenger of Satan, to torment me. ⁸Three times I pleaded with the Lord to take it away from me. ⁹But he said to me, 'My grace is sufficient for you, for my power is made perfect in weakness.' Therefore I will boast all the more gladly about my weaknesses, so that Christ's power may rest on me. ¹⁰That is why, for Christ's sake, I delight in weaknesses, in insults, in hardships, in persecutions, in difficulties. For when I am weak, then I am strong."*

Paul's request was answered by the giving of grace. He received God's own empowerment to labor with the infirmity in order to glorify Christ in his own weakness. Also, Paul's companion and fellow laborer was not healed of his illness (2 Timothy 4: 20 NIV).

I have prayed specifically for healing of my physical infirmity for many years, and was answered in different ways by God in much the same way Paul's request was answered. Strength and grace was given for each day's journey. Days of grace became for me months and years of God's genial care.

This is my assessment with my limited understanding of what God is doing in my life.

January 2002, I reached my fifth decade of life without much of a celebration. We went to a pub and had dinner that evening. None of us had found employment as yet and we survived by cautiously spending our limited resources.

Living in Leicester was a short experience, less than a year. While unemployed, my brother informed me that I could register with the social service to receive unemployment benefit. So, I did. I received assistance every two weeks until a job was found.

Janice found work in her field with Leicester Royal Infirmary in our third month of residency and I found part- time employment as a substitute/assistant teacher with Hamilton Community College four months into the New Year.

We went to several churches for a while and settled on Braunstone United Reform Church. We participated in the church's life and were given preaching opportunities. I sensed that the time and place for starting a new fellowship was not in that city and continued to pray for God's leading.

We were requested to serve the London fellowship from which we severed our leadership position three consecutive times, to conduct home-going funeral services for the elderly who passed away. While in London we stayed with Pernelle in his residential flat.

Sometime in June, Janice was asked by the employer-to-be in Florida, to take several English exams. Two were done in a London testing site while the third was schedule in Paris, France. We went to Paris on a rainy Friday evening. From the airport we traveled by train to our destination and could not find the hotel we had made our reservations. We eventually walked into a hotel that accommodated us on the same street with the testing site.

We got a taxi the next morning to take us to the site about a half-hour ride and arrived on time for the scheduled test. On completion, we toured the area on foot, had lunch, picked up a few souvenirs and returned to the hotel in the evening. Next day, we left the hotel at checkout time, found our way to the train station by taxi, paid our fare and boarded the train to the airport. Since our flight was later in the afternoon, we relaxed until our flight was called to take us back to Leicester.

Near the end of July, we were asked to take biometrics tests in preparation for visa interview in London. In August, we had our interview at the US Embassy for entry visas; but were delayed in receiving it due in part to a certificate Janice should have received from an organization in Philadelphia. When we finally received the document, and rescheduled the interview, Pernelle had just passed his twenty-first birthday on August 10th. He was denied a visa because the interviewer said the system automatically deprived him due to his age. Though disappointed, we were content in the fact that we were able to give him the opportunity to become independent. He was already living on his own and working with periodic social assistance.

Before leaving Leicester, I was hospitalized for about five days with congestion. While there, I was assigned a case social worker. Her responsibility was to engage me on her visits on proper use of medication, information on the disease, and shared with me articles and websites where additional information could be found. She also suggested that I may find the Cycle Cell Anemia/Thalassemia Association helpful as a support group.

With entry visa, we made travel arrangements for October 2nd 2002. We placed the house up for sale with a realtor on a ninety-day contract. We determined what we needed to take with us and began downsizing. From what we sold, we bought seven hundred US dollars as travel money. The car was put up for sale since the shipper advised it would not worth the while to send it across the ocean.

We got through security and waited for our flight at the designated gate. Our gate was called at 8.00AM and we boarded. Not long after take-off, I fell asleep due to being up almost all night. When they served the first meal Janice woke me.

Crossing the Atlantic from England to Florida on British Airways seemed much longer than when we first made the trip from Chicago. New anxieties began sprouting in my mind: suppose I'm not able to find a job in the next ninety-days? What if the job Janice is about to take up is not permanent and will be just for the two years of contract? Would it not have been the better choice for her to go it alone for that short time? Suppose the house does not sell for the asking price, how then would we clear the rest of the mortgage?

Staring through the aircraft's window closest to me alleviated my inner musings and concerns for a while. Janice just kept on reading her book. Again, I may have dropped off to sleep. An hour before landing, food was again served.

At 2:20 PM EST we landed at Miami International Airport. We negotiated our way by following the lead of others toward the Immigration services. When we got to the officer and handed in our documents, we were drawn aside into another room to retake fingerprints and pictures. This was a long and unexpected wait. On completion, the officer indicated that our Green Cards were being processed and would get to us within thirty-days at the address provided.

With authorization stamps in our passports, we were shown out of the office and told where we would find our luggage. We found our bags and called a taxi; trusting that the cab driver would know exactly where we were heading, and would take us there directly. All we had was a street address and no one from the employment agency came to walk us through this process. When we communicated with them prior to leaving, we were instructed that taxi fare from the airport to Kendall would be about thirty dollars. When we actually arrive at the address, the total was forty- five dollars due in part to our delay in the immigration office and heavy afternoon traffic.

We removed our stuff from the taxi, took them to the upstairs apartment, and waited for someone to come and let us in. A lady came with keys and opens the apartment for us. She walked us through with instructions for telephone, use of electrical appliances, garbage disposal, and such things as she remembered in relation to the apartment. She instructed how to get to the nearest bus stop, where to do laundry, where to shop until we were properly settled. In all of this, she kept reminding us that three months will pass very quickly and by the end of the time we needed to find our own permanent place. Then she left.

Another person came around six O'clock and took us to shop at Publix Supermarket. We picked-up a few things which surprisingly came up to over one hundred dollars. We were happy for the shopping favor since we did not have to take the bus, and so, when we got back home we were able to unpack, eat, and relax for the evening. We thanked God for His grace and protection and asked for wisdom and guidance for the days ahead.

Next day, Janice reported to her new employer for new instructions. Orientation to the hospital would start and run for three weeks; after which work will begin in earnest; and on the completion of the first three months, medical insurance coverage would be provided.

I began walking around the complex extending my range in all directions with time. I observed where the Public Library, a Bank, small shops and offices were located. I found also the location of the Kendall Community Church of God on 112th street. When we actually connected the phone, we were able to give our address and location to extended friends and family.

The rest of October flew by quickly and by the start of November, I returned to Leicester to sign new papers for the sale of our house. The new buyer did not want the electrical appliances and some furniture, thus, I had to get rid of them. I checked in with my hematologist and was transfused two units of red blood cells. Checking in with Janice by phone two weeks after leaving, I learned that our shipment had arrived and she had rented a storage bin for storage.

The house did not sell immediately even though I spent almost four weeks waiting for the buyer to come through with his loan. So, I purchased my ticket and asked my brother Phillex to sell my car.

On my return to Miami, we opened our first checking/saving account with the neighborhood Executive National Bank; because it was within walking distance from home, and if we were going to find another apartment in the area, it would serve us well. The account was opened with the equivalent of five hundred pounds which I had withdrawn from our account in England; money from Janice' last pay.

Christmas came and we spent it quietly. We had walked to church a few Sundays. We were introduced to Pastor Daniel Harden and other members of staff with time. We learned that Pastor Harden was about to retire and If my credentials checked out with the Florida State Credentials Committee, I could be called on to fill the pulpit occasionally. This gave me some hope of earning my way, but I needed to make the connections with the state to lodge my papers.

In January 2003, we moved from the Landings at 8741 SW 94th Street, Miami, FL 33176 to 8475 SW 94th Street, Apt 207 E, Miami, Fl 33156. This was a one bed apartment and cost five hundred dollars per month. Included was water usage and we paid for electricity. We moved some of our stuff from storage to furnish the apartment; it was comfortable for a while. Like the Landings, it also provided a coin laundry. But unlike the Landings, this was a noisy place, especially in the evenings when the other occupants of other apartments came in from work. We could hear people talking and cars coming and going out of the driveway all hours of the night. Janice's shift was mostly three-to-eleven and I would walk over to the hospital to accompany her home at eleven.

I bought a step down transformer so that I could use the computer I brought with me from England. With cable, we were able to use the internet connected by AT&T. In contacting the credentialing office of the Florida Church of God, I was instructed to submit my ordination papers and references from last ministry position. This I did using mail connections for the Tottenham Church in London.

On completion of her ninety-day probation, Janice was asked to sign up for health insurance, which she did with the company's insurer, United Health. This enabled us to find medical, dental and vision care physicians in the network. I found and registered with Dr. Michael Troner, hematologist at the same hospital.

On my first appointment, I took what records I had and went through a number of blood tests, x-rays, and scans of the chest. From that first meeting, I sensed that he was quite caring and knowledgeable of the disease and was up- to-date on latest practice and care procedures. I am still his patient. We also found Andrea Diamond's dental practice and signed on with her for our dental care. Our vision doctor was Dr. James Segal of MedEye Associates; he recently passed away. All three were Jewish physicians.

The end of January 2003, I was credentialed by the state to do ministry. I preached my first sermon on the first Sunday in February and was asked to fill the pulpit every other Sunday for a twelve week period. During this time as well, the house was finally sold and the bank paid. The solicitor wired the remaining funds to our account with Executive National on the tenth of February.

We decided it was time to purchase a car. We got to know the bus routes very well to get to where we desired, but it was time consuming. We scouted the newspapers to get an idea of the cost and spoke to friends as to what auto insurance was going to be. We decided that we would look for a pre-owned vehicle in good condition. After much prayer and searching the newspapers, we took the bus to Hyundai showroom on US1South one morning in April. There we were shown several vehicles and we settled on a 2002 maroon *Elantra* with fifteen thousand miles. It was reasonably priced. We were happy with our purchase and before driving off; we thanked God and asked for protection as we drove home just in time for Janice to get to work.

I enquired of a principal, a member of the Kendall fellowship, the procedure for accessing a teaching position. She walked me through the process and gave me the directions to the Miami-Dade Public School Office. The process was not as exactly or easy as she had explained to me. The office personnel that dealt with me took the application, sat me down to write an essay on *"Why I believe I would be an effective teacher."* On completion, she looked at my credentials I presented and then informed me that I had another step: I needed to have my certification evaluated by Joseph Silney – a company that they recommend – to applicants whose educational credentials were gained outside of the US. With that information, I called up the office and found that I needed to have transcripts sent to them from West Indies Theological College and Anderson University School of Theology, respectively. On the internet, I found the names of the registrars and the cost for the requests. Money orders were purchased and posted, and in the space of four weeks, transcripts were sent to the authorized body. Another three weeks would elapse before I received my evaluation. I took the evaluation back to the School Board office and was again told that my qualifications will only allow me to start as a substitute teacher.

"How does the system of substituting works?" I asked.

"You are given a registration number and schools that need you will call you either before, or on the day that they need you to come in," she explained.

To be entered into the system, she continued, I needed to be finger-printed and drug tested. When these were done, I was registered and within the space of two days I was called to begin work at Leisure City K-8, in Homestead where David Brooks was Principal.

The purchase of our first home came about when the noise and constant confusion within the complex became unbearable. Our lease was for a year but the area was not conducive to our happiness. We began looking for a home. Mrs. Jose Kendall was a realtor and member of the church and she offered to help us find a place within our prearranged budget. The homes she had in her portfolio were very nice but a bit out of our financial range. Yet, we were very appreciative for her assistance and exposure to what was available. What we had in mind was three beds, two baths and a garage home for modest living.

We were helped by another realtor Armando Barrios. He was not a pushy guy who just wanted to unload the first house he had in his portfolio. He took time to work with us to make sure we got the best value for our money in an acceptable quiet area that we desired. He suggested that homes in Homestead would be more in line pricewise than in Kendall and further north of Kendall. Nevertheless, we had to look at quite a few houses before we landed the right one.

Our mortgage company, Home Financing Inc. was a joy to work with. We met Robert Wheeler who walked us through the process. He informed us that usually they would not lend money to persons who had such limited credit history since we have just been in the country for six months. Yet, he approved us for the amount we wanted. We were asked to have a down payment of twenty percent of the loan for fifteen years at five percent interest per annum.

The home we found was a corner lot situated at 140 NE 19th Street, (Downer Palms) Homestead, FL33030. It was built in nineteen-seventy-six but was just renovated with a new roof, windows and doors; on the inside with new bathrooms and kitchen. It was freshly painted inside and out and was in move-in ready condition. The listed price was one hundred and forty-five thousand and we made the offer to the seller on the same day we viewed it.

We gave notification to our landlord of our intention to move before the lease was up. He wished us well but also reminded us that we will still have to pay for the remaining months until the year was completed.

We signed our final papers on Friday June thirteenth and got our water and light connected on the same afternoon.

Moving occurred on the following day Saturday, June fourteenth. The moving company came at around seven o'clock and packed the furniture and other boxed stuff in the van. I packed our clothing in the back seat of the car. We then drove to the storage bin and emptied it. We arrived at our new home around eleven thirty and unpacked everything in the garage; paid the movers and began rearranging things for living. It took a few months for us to settle and furnish all the rooms.

We invited friends and some church members for our house warming in September. Pastor Norris and Vassell Ferris came from Atlanta, Georgia and did the blessing. He used the scripture from the Old Testament 1Samuel 7:12 "...*He called the place Ebenezer, saying, to this point has the Lord helped us.*" And from Romans 14:8 "*If we live, we live for the Lord; and if we die, we die for the Lord. So, whether we live or die, we belong to the Lord.*" This was an excellent devotional of encouragement for us starting out on a new adventure in our new home.

Going back to college was a challenge. I registered with Miami-Dade College at the Kendall campus to pursue AA in education after passing the GED. I received financial Aid in the form of a Pell Grant for the two-year program, it was greatly welcomed. The most challenging area of that study was mathematics for which I had received extra help one hour in the afternoon per week from a fine teacher Melanie Porter from the Kendall Church. When she was unavailable, her brother Matthew who is also a fine teacher would assist me. Biology, chemistry, physics, and statistics were also difficult but manageable. On completion of the two years, I registered with FIU (Florida International University) for the teaching certificate. The first semester was rough and I decided to check out Barry University's program in teaching.

Barry program met my needs since the classes were taught in cohorts. I was able to access student loans to pay for each semester and racked up a very large debt at the end of the process. On graduation, I received the Bachelors of Science with a major in Elementary Education with English for Second Language Students (ESOL) Endorsement. This certification helped me to find permanent work. I also continued study with the same university for the Master's program in reading. This also took two years and I completed it on time.

Going back to 2004, we began having home bible study with an eye to launching a new fellowship in Homestead. For this venture, we attended many church planting conferences, training camps, and seminars; some put on by our church state body, others by interdenominational organizations.

The prime purpose of the intended new fellowship was stated in our Mission Statement as follows from the New International Version:

- To share the good news of Jesus Christ – *evangelism*
- (Matt. 28: 18-20)
- To celebrate God's love in Christ – *worship* (Phil 2: 9-11)

- To care for each other through service – *fellowship* (2Cor 8:1-5)
- To live like Christ – *discipleship* (John 18: 12-21)
- To study God's word – *enlightenment* (2 Tim 2: 15).

We started with five families that attended faithfully each Wednesday evening. These families would in time become the founding members of Homestead Community Church of God Inc. This was God's answer to my prayer and desire not to be working *for* a church but to shape others into a fellowship of cooperation and mission to the community.

Also at this time, Janice transferred from Kendall Baptist to Homestead Baptist which cut travel time by an hour.

We had our first public worship on the first Sunday in January, 2005 at 2:00 PM held at The Homestead YMCA community room. We had set up our organization and registered with the state as an independent religious, social and educational non-profit.

We applied for 501 (3) (C) status with IRS and got approved. Brother Linford Codling was our Chairperson and for our launch, he procured a sound system. His wife Yvonne was our treasurer; Brother Craig Aquart was my associate pastor/assistant, and his wife Patrice was our visual aid projectionist and later, second treasurer. Sis. Toni Henry-Green was our secretary and my wife Janice was her assistant. Faithful members were Sis. Maureen and her family; Sis. Paulette and her family; Sis. Julienne and her family along with Sis. Nelle Jacobs and her family.

Bro. Phillmore Hallpike was our musician on a portable organ that we purchased and Pastor Norris Ferris and Lady Vassell Ferris from the Community Church of God, Atlanta, Georgia was our guest speaker.

The sermon was clearly appropriate and challenging from Acts 2: 41-47 KJV under the theme, *The Attributes of a Local Church*. We were challenged to *proclaim* the gospel; to *fellowship* as they did in the early church; to *share* what we have received with the community; to constantly *pray* for the needs of the community; to *worship* God with all our being; and to *witness* to the authority of God's transforming power in Christ. We had support from the Kendall Community Church with Pastor William Ferguson and members in attendance.

The greatest joy and surprise of the day was the arrival of my Mom who came especially for the occasion. My sister Julienne had previously moved from Shreveport, Louisiana, to

Florida the year before. She was recruited by a nursing agency and brought to Louisiana on contract, but issues developed that prevented her from making a formidable contribution. She lived with us for four months before finding her own apartment at the Caribbean Blvd Apartment complex. Mom stayed with Julienne until she was ready to go back home in December of 2008.

In 2006, we bought our second home in Waterstone community – 3965 NE 12th Drive, Homestead, FL 33030. This was a new construction of four bed/three baths home with over two thousand square feet under air condition. Looking back, this was a real bad decision.

To begin, it was a gated community with a number of restrictions and community fees. Second, we did the purchase at a bad time just before the market crashed with no down-payment. Third, we worked with people we did not know and who did not care to make clear adjustable rates. Fourth, parking space was limited to two cars only on the property and there was no place for visitors to park. Each year, the association fee went up by about ten percent.

The intent we had in mind when we made this decision to purchase was, we would rent out our first home and the rent would pay the first mortgage and the remainder would help to off-set some of the mortgage for the second home. It worked for the first two years but the second mortgage kept going up until it became unmanageable.

The church stayed at the YMCA until July of 2005. There were two reasons for wanting to move: first, we had to move our stuff in and out each time we used the spot. Sometimes the previous user left the space in a mess and we coming after had to clean it before setting up. Second, we needed a bigger space for growth and we felt that if such a place could be found, we would be able to change worship time from afternoon to morning. We found a nice spot in a strip mall – 70 NE Homestead Blvd. The rent was challenging but by grace, manageable on a one year contract. God helped us to stay there for the first six years of our existence.

We saw slow numerical growth each year but within that time, we grew spiritually and financially through the consistent teaching and giving of the membership. We developed youth and children's programs which enhanced the desire and enthusiasm of the church. The children and youth began inviting their friends and gradually the parent would come occasionally.

We were blessed with the presence of Pastor Roger Ramage and family from around 2007 until his retirement to Ocala, Florida. He was not only our musician but also a gifted preacher and teacher.

In the summer of 2007, we were pleased to have family members from Janice's side come to stay with us for two months. Her Mom Gwendolyn Richardson with one granddaughter; and Aunt Jarvis with two granddaughters.

It was fun on some days to have them. We took them on a four days' trip to Disney World which they enjoyed immensely, as well as to other places of interest in Miami.

In January 2008, we were notified by the Baptist lawyer that we could apply for Naturalization which they offered to do for us at an unreasonable cost. We determined to get it done ourselves and so we did with the help of Lindford's secretary, Aijah. She filled the forms online and printed them out for us. We posted them with the other required documents, and waited. We received a package of study material and an interview date in May. By June we had our interview and in July we had our Naturalization ceremony.

In September also, while I was doing my internship at Redlands Elementary School, Janice had to be rushed to the emergency room at the Homestead Hospital with stomach pain. We went there the Sunday evening at around six-thirty. When she was admitted, it was about ten-thirty. Diagnosis: obstruction of the large intestine. Surgery was the only way to correct the blockage which was done around 2:00 AM on Monday morning.

My Mom died in Antigua on June eleventh, 2009. She succumbed to complications of pneumonia at the age of ninety-four. She became very restless at the end of 2008 and requested that she return home. She probably wanted to die in Antigua rather than in Florida. Julienne took her home in December and by June she passed away. We travelled there mid-June to plan funeral services. Her funeral services were held on June 27th at the Valley Anglican Church where she attended in her youthful years in Bolans. Her passing did not adversely affect me in that through our times together, I got to know her faith and trust in Christ. She made her confession and peace with God. Though there was sorrow, it was not of the kind whereby there is no knowledge of her eternal place in the kingdom of God.

We stayed in Antigua for Janelle's wedding which was held on July fourth. Janelle is my niece and Julienne's first of three daughters.

On our stay there, we also had to get from the High Court the Judge's Order for the adoption of Pernelle. We had never gotten a copy, which was requested by INS to process his visa application. We had asked a relative there to look into getting it done, but unsuccessfully. We spent one afternoon at the office before Mom's funeral and explained our need to the clerk. Happily, the person who was assigned to make the search was a friend of ours and she made the extra effort to find the file and make the copy. She called us a few days later and instructed that we had to pay the stamp duty of fifty dollars which we did and on the Friday before leaving the Island, we collected it from the department.

On our return to Florida, we received from the state church an invitation to become fully incorporated into the organization. We were approved for provisional status In September of that year.

There were three highlights of 2011. The first was moving the church's location back to 140 NE 19th Street, where, we renovated the garage into our worship center. We did this in order to take advantage of the down-turn in the housing market with an eye to purchase our own space. We saw a few properties that we could have converted into our permanent church location within the budget that we had. We found one such location at 90 NW 22nd Street, Miami, FL 33032. This was half acre lot with a structure of twenty-two hundred square feet. The interior of the structure was gutted and the cost was eighty-five thousand dollars. The owner provided a fifty thousand dollar loan to us as we paid down thirty-five thousand with two years to pay back, which we did, at five percent interest. We thought that since the interior was gutted we did not need permits from the city to begin work which we did.

We were cited by Code Enforcement department of the city for doing work on the interior of the building without proper permits. We paid our fine and applied for the relevant permits to have the work done. Unfortunately, the city kept moving the requirements for permitting the renovations. For an entire year, they sent us around in circles, creating frustration. In time, we had to sell the property.

The second major highlight was the loss of our home at 3965 NE 12th Drive. The payment had become unmanageable and after several attempts to get the mortgage modified, we determine that it was not worth the hassle. Since the tenant was a good paying one, we decided to short sale the second home and rent a place until the contract was terminated.

We eventually moved by renting a two-bed apartment in Venetian Gardens at 1300 SE 31st Court, Apt 102, Homestead, FL 33035. We then placed in storage our excess furniture, books and utensils.

Finally, my sister Elvira passed away in St. Thomas, Virgin Islands, where she lived for most of her adult life. She was the first daughter of our mother and I was asked to eulogies her at her funeral service. I drew attention to our relationship since she was our caretaker most of the time when we were infants and when Mom was at work. Personally, she cared for me during my often illness and when I needed to get to the hospital or clinic for treatment. When she migrated to St. Thomas she was mindful of our need and would post food and clothing packages on a regular basis. My first high school uniform shirts she provided along with my leather shoes. She lived with a kind gentle heart of compassion; she shared her limited resources generously; she served her community with civic pride through volunteering to pick-up and distributes meals to the poor from the Salvation Army – the church she attended in her adult life. She had a strong faith and worked tirelessly for her children to do the same.

> *"Redeemer God, sometimes You allow tragedy, sickness, ailment, death or even what we consider bad things into our lives, not so much to make us doubt Your love for us, but more importantly, to draw us more deeply into Your gracious care. So now I pray in the words of the song, Help me then in every tribulation, So to trust Thy promises, O Lord, That I lose not faith's sweet consolation; Offered me within Thy holy Word. Help me, Lord, when toil and trouble meeting, E'er to take, as from a father's hand, One by one, the days, the Moments fleeting, Till I reach the promised land[3]. Lord God, grant me understanding to interpret what you are doing in my life, so that I may walk in your way with confidence, assurance and faith; shine the light of your truth upon my path. Help me to walk in that revealed truth each day."* Amen.

---

[3] Lyrics of third verse of Day by Day, written by Karolina W. Sandell-Berge 1880. Lyrics are in public domain. *www.hymnsuntogod.org/Hymns-PD/ZZ- CompletePDHymnList.html.*

Chapter Seven

I PRAYED FOR HEALING AND HE GAVE ME AN OPEN FUTURE

Jeremiah 29:11 NIV makes a futuristic prediction to an exiled people in Babylon. It says of God, *"For I know the plans I have for you, declares the Lord; plans to prosper you and not to harm you, plans to give you hope and a future."* The background of this verse is a nation exiled in Babylon. Jeremiah had previously warned the nation that they were in eminent danger of being cast into exile because of their abandonment of God's righteousness (Jeremiah 25:1-11 NIV). Eventually, the warning became reality, and he then got another word from God to encourage the exiled nation to remind them that God will provide a future and hope.

This passage has special significance for me as I endeavored to listen and practice the will of God in my life. Such prophecies are never tied to the original historical context but are applicable to all people for all time. The passage not only speaks to a lost nation but more specifically to each individual making up that nation. Like each participating

Israelite, I too have made mistakes that have angered God. And I have paid for them over time just like the Israelites, yet, God's word to me through Jeremiah stands: *"I know the plans I have for you…plans for a future and a hope."*

At the end of 2011 – my fifty-ninth year of life, I wondered how much time I had left to live to see that future hope. My Thalassemia was not improving, and my reliance on frequent transfusions was becoming critical. I became introspective more so now than before; in my preaching and teaching I spoke on how prepared we must be to meet our God at any time. It was a time of soul-searching for finding out my sins of omission as well as sins of commission. I stayed up late at nights pondering where I have failed or hurt anyone, deprived, defrauded, or in any way bring shame and dishonor, with perspective to finding ways to make it right. The only issue that came up before me was my reneged promise to go back and serve the Zion Church of God, Antigua. And I had already done what was possible at the time to make amends.

January 18th, 2012 rolled around, and I was sixty years of age. No grand party was pursued. The day was spent quietly in reflection and in the evening we went out for dinner.

I was teaching part time at two schools (Mavericks High School, a charter establishment and Redlands Middle) on short term contracts, endeavoring to improve students reading skills. I guess the stress of leaving home early in the morning and getting back late each evening was too much for my physique.

The next five years had quite a few health challenges. In October of 2012, I had the first heart surgery to remove my bad aortic valve. The cardiologist explained that over the years, the valve was overworked and became inefficient by not closing properly. Surgery was successful, but blood clots accumulated around the new valve and I was rushed back to Surgery twenty-hours after the first to remove them. Four years later (12-06-2016), I was back for a TAVR on the same valve which began malfunctioning. On 24th May 2017, test on the heart showed weakness in the lower portion of heart muscles and so, a pacemaker was recommended to strengthen and prevent a sudden stop.

After the first surgery in twenty-twelve, I was instructed and made determined effort to slow down. I explained to the church my condition and suggested taking some time off. Pastor Craig graciously and effectively held things together for three months. I gradually began taking part but utilized many of the members' talents in worship and preaching.

Also, in 2012 Janice was accepted in a BSN program sponsored by her employer; which was offered at Barry University. Because it was part-time, graduation was three years after.

I fully retired in 2016 both from the school system and the Homestead Church of God, which we closed. When I closed my fellowship, it took us about fourteen months to find another fellowship to be permanently associated with. We visited a great number of local churches and settled on South Dade Baptist Church.

Now that I've lived to become retired from active employment, I'm able to make a conscious evaluation of my life. I've had a wonderful *springtime* in my first twenty years of life. My *summer* years were hectic covering the next twenty years of family life, study and work. The *fall* or *autumn* of my life brought increased health challenges; and now that I'm approaching the *winter* years, I am confident that the same God, who walked with me through all the previous years, will continue to guide me the rest of the way. As the ancient Rabbis say, and I paraphrase, *"One must enjoy the interest of his or her righteousness in this life and the deposit remains for them in the hereafter."* I have truly enjoyed my life and will continue to do so until the end.

I've had a wonderful and blessed life to this point. What's next? I will spend the rest of my time, whether it is a day, a week, a month or many years, according to God's plan; in volunteering with a worthy organization that is in line with my Christian philosophy and values; reading good books, writing, photography, learning the piano keyboard, and possibly some painting. My future is still in God's hands.

> *Master of the Universe, Creator and sustainer of life, I thank You this day for my existence and the quality of life You grace and mercy have afforded me through Jesus Christ my Savior. Master of the Universe, Creator and sustainer of Life, You have demonstrated Your compassionate care toward us in the abundance of material resources You put at our disposal. But You have also made it very clear that we do not live by material things alone. Master of the Universe, Creator and sustainer of Life, You have provided in Jesus Christ Your Son and our Savior, the spiritual resources in great abundance that we might live unto eternal life; You have given us an*

abundance of grace, peace, The word, the Holy Spirit, the Fellowship of the Church, patience and longsuffering, forgiveness and tolerance.

Master of the Universe, Creator and sustainer of Life, enable us to be forever mindful that by offering even a cup of cold water to the needy, even in welcoming the little ones among us in Your name, doing good to widows, orphans, protecting the weak and vulnerable, visiting those who are sick or imprisoned – that we are building-up treasures in Heaven. Master of the Universe, Creator and sustainer of Life, help us to make your Kingdom's goal our life's work whether we are rich or poor, full of health or weaken by ailment, so that we may boldly say, "The Lord is our Helper." Amen.

Storyline through Photos

My Dad: circa 1960. Charles Elias Caleb Moitt.
Born June 7th 1917, Died Feb. 4th 1983.

Below: My Mom in 2008 in Florida.
Born: August 31st 1915. Died June 11th 2009

My sisters Julienne & Daisymae and myself, circa 1956

Official Customs &
Excise Uniform 1974

Customs Course
JJ, 1975

Certificate of
Completion

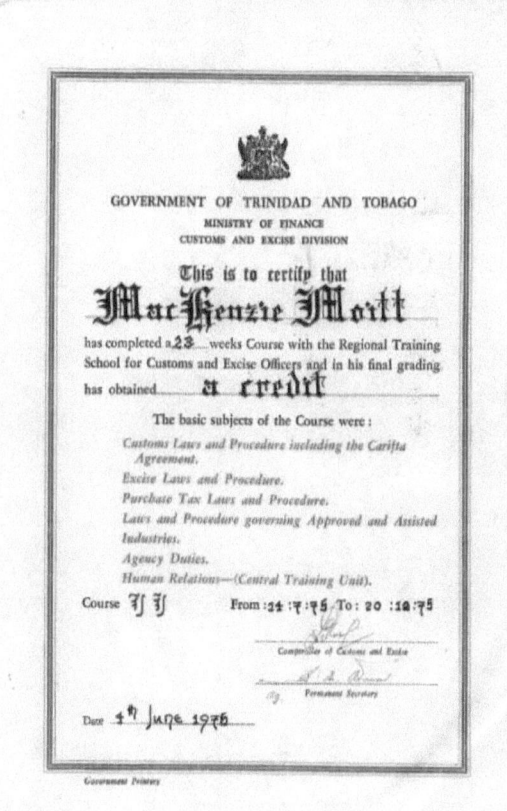

Wedding Day: September 29th, 1977.

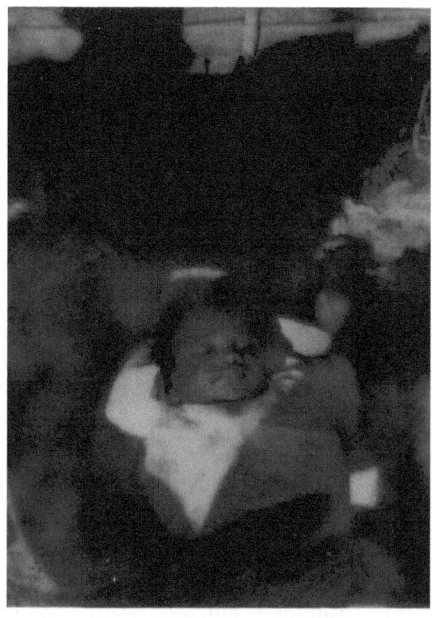

Baby Pernelle before adoption 1982

Work day at WITC 1984

Above: 1985 Graduation at WITC with Mom.

Below: Commencement at School of Theology, Anderson University, 1993. R to L: Julienne, Janice, myself and Pernelle.

American Bible Society award for outstanding achievement
in Biblical Studies 1995

June, 1995 leaving Anderson

R to L: Pernelle, Joseph Smythe, Janice and myself

Installation as pastors at Community Church of God,
London September, 1995

Citation and Certificate of Excellence for achievement in World Literature from Miami-Dade College 2004

HCOG Launch invitation card 2005
(Designed and created by Craig Aquart).

Left to right: Janice, Julienne, Mom and myself after Worship 2007

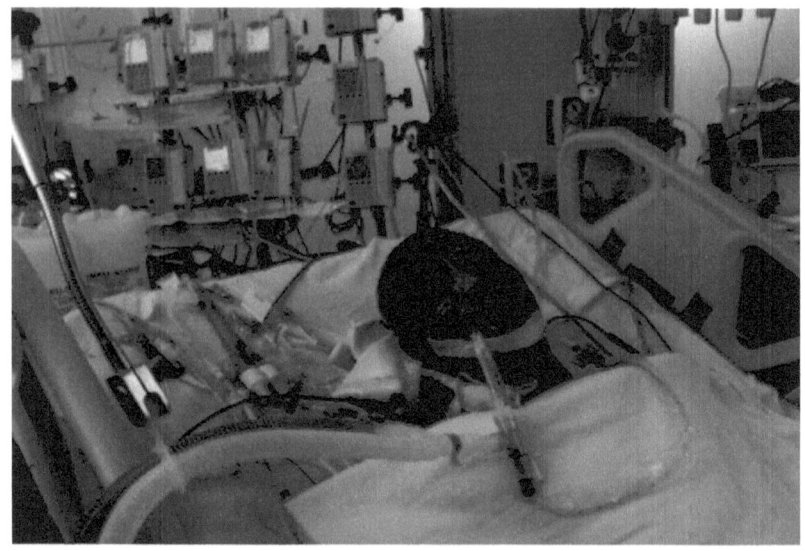

2012 First surgery: Intensive care room.

2017 Retirement Cruise, shore excursion, France.

www.ingramcontent.com/pod-product-compliance
Lightning Source LLC
Chambersburg PA
CBHW030113100526
44591CB00009B/388